C000075624

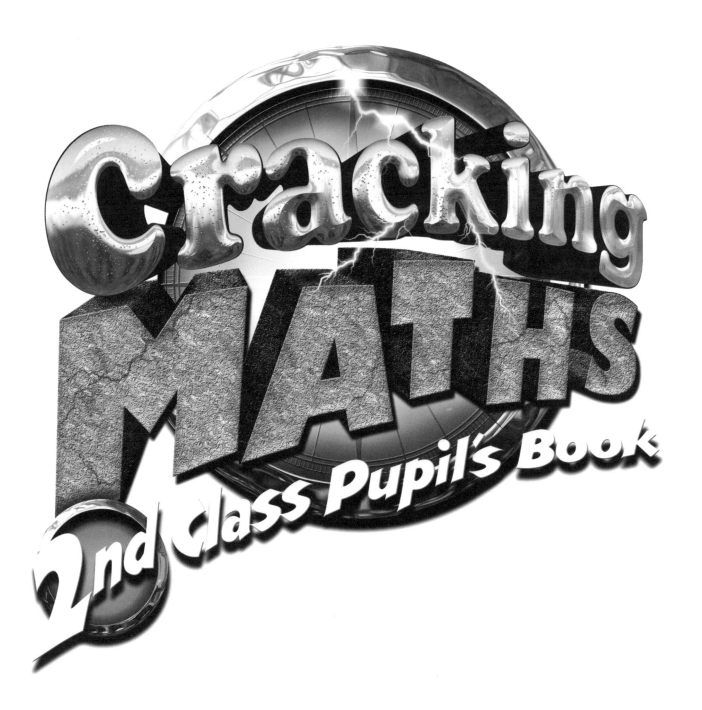

Cracking MATHS
2nd Class Pupil's Book

Majella O'Connor, Aishling Doyle,
Joan Gilligan, Carmel Kelly, Catherine Knight

GILL EDUCATION

Gill Education
Hume Avenue
Park West
Dublin 12
www.gilleducation.ie

Gill Education is an imprint of M.H. Gill & Co.

ISBN: 978 07171 54210

© Majella O'Connor, Aishling Doyle, Joan Gilligan, Carmel Kelly, Catherine Knight 2014

Design: Outburst Design and Richard Jervis
Internal illustrations: Derry Dillon
Technical drawings: MPS Limited
Cover illustration: www.designbos.ie
Consultant editor in mathematics curriculum and pedagogy: Betty Stoutt
Mathematics consultant: Oliver Hyde

The paper used in this book comes from the wood pulp of sustainably managed forests.

All rights reserved.
No part of this publication may be copied, reproduced or transmitted in any form or by any means, without written permission of the publishers or else under the terms of any licence permitting limited copying issued by the Irish Copyright Licensing Agency.

Any links to external websites should not be construed as an endorsement by Gill Education of the content or view of the linked material.

For permission to reproduce photographs, the authors and publisher gratefully acknowledge the following:

© Alamy: 141 (butter); © Shutterstock: 38, 40, 48, 52, 107, 108, 109, 110, 111, 112, 113, 139, 140, 141, 142, 144, 145, 146, 147, 149.

The authors and publisher have made every effort to trace all copyright holders, but if any has been inadvertently overlooked we would be pleased to make the necessary arrangement at the first opportunity.

Contents

1. Look Back

1. a) How many?

   Estimate ☐ Count ☐

   b) How many?

   Estimate ☐ Count ☐

2. a) Draw 12 balloons

   b) Draw 17 triangles

3. **What number comes before?**

 19   ☐ 45   ☐ 81

4. **What number comes after?**

16 ☐   32 ☐   68 ☐

5. **What number comes between?**

4 ☐ 6   11 ☐ 13   46 ☐ 48   37 ☐ 39   69 ☐ 71

6. **How many altogether?**

a)

☐ + ☐ = ☐

b)

☐ + ☐ = ☐

c)

☐ + ☐ = ☐

7. 7 + 4 = ☐   9 + 3 = ☐   7 + 9 = ☐   11 + 4 = ☐   14 + 6 = ☐

Curriculum Objective:
To revise concepts that were explored in 1st class.

8.

4   +   1   +   4   = ☐

7   +   3   +   3   = ☐

4   +   5   +   4   = ☐

8   +   2   +   6   = ☐

9.   6 + 1 + 4 = ☐   4 + 4 + 5 = ☐   5 + 7 + 5 = ☐   2 + 5 + 8 = ☐

10. a) How many left?   b) How many left?

8 − 3 = ☐   13 − 5 = ☐

11. a)   7 − 5 = ☐   9 − 3 = ☐   11 − 0 = ☐   13 − 2 = ☐

    b) 18 − 4 = ☐   16 − 8 = ☐   14 − 5 = ☐   17 − 10 = ☐

12. a) 6 + 2 = 2 + ☐   b) 12 + 3 = 3 + ☐   c) 9 + 8 = ☐ + 9

💡 Add the units first.

13.

t u	t u	t u	t u	t u	t u	t u	t u
1 7	1 2	2 4	1 6	3 2	1 0	4 3	3 4
+ 1 1	+ 1 3	+ 1 2	+ 2 1	+ 1 3	+ 2 8	+ 4 6	+ 5

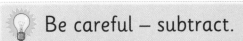
14.

t u	t u	t u	t u
1 7	1 8	1 6	2 3
+ 1 6	+ 1 8	+ 2 9	+ 2 8

15.

t u	t u	t u	t u
5 5	2 7	3 7	8 8
– 3 2	– 1 0	– 6	– 1 5

16. **Tick** ✓ **the box under each shape that is cut in half.**

17. **Name the 2-D shapes**

square semi-circle triangle circle rectangle

a) _____   b) _____   c) _____   d) _____   e) _____

18. **Name the 3-D shapes**

cuboid   sphere   cube   cylinder

a) _____   b) _____   c) _____   d) _____

19. **Draw the hands to show the time.**

a) 7 o'clock   b) 11 o'clock   c) half past one   d) half past nine

20. **Write the time.**

a)    b)   c)   d)

_____   _____   _____

21. **How much money is in each box?**

a)

| c |

b)

| c |

c)

| c |

22. **Draw the coins to make the correct amount.**

a)

8c

b)

24c

c)

49c

23. **Write the correct word.**

same   lighter   heavier

a) The oranges are _____ than the grapes.
b) The carrots are _____ than the potatoes.
c) The crayons weigh the _____ as the pencils.

24. **Write the correct word.**

longest   shortest   longer   shorter

a) The chain is _____ than the worm.
b) The rope is _____ than the snake.
c) The snake is the _____.
d) The worm is the _____.

25. **Write the correct word.**

cup   bucket   mug   jug   pool

a) The _____ holds the least amount of water.
b) The _____ holds the most water.
c) The jug holds less water than the _____ .
d) The _____ holds less water than the jug.
e) The mug holds more water than the _____ .

---

26. **Write the numeral on each flag.**

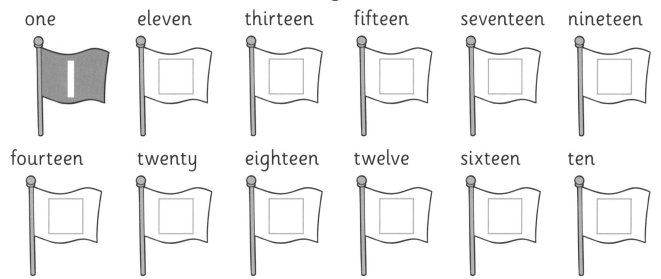

one   eleven   thirteen   fifteen   seventeen   nineteen

fourteen   twenty   eighteen   twelve   sixteen   ten

---

27. **Match the numeral to the word.**

11	seventeen
15	twelve
17	fourteen
14	eleven
12	fifteen

19	thirteen
16	twenty
13	sixteen
18	nineteen
20	eighteen

28. **Write the word.**

11 = _____   13 = _____   15 = _____

17 = _____   19 = _____   12 = _____

14 = _____   16 = _____   20 = _____

2. Addition 1

What do you notice when you add zero?

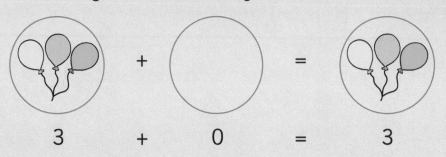

3 + 0 = 3

1. **Add zero to these numbers.**

4 + 0 = ☐   6 + 0 = ☐   12 + 0 = ☐   15 + 0 = ☐

13 + 0 = ☐   0 + 3 = ☐   0 + 18 = ☐   0 + 4 = ☐

2.
```
  16     14      7      9     17      0      0       0       0       0
+  0    + 0    + 0    + 0    + 0    + 2    + 8    + 19    + 11    + 15
____   ____   ____   ____   ____   ____   ____   _____   _____   _____
```

What do you notice when you add one?

3 + 1 = 4

3.
3 + 1 = ☐

5 + 1 = ☐

9 + 1 = ☐

16 + 1 = ☐

Strand: Number
Curriculum Objectives:
Develop an understanding of addition by combining or partitioning sets;
develop and recall mental strategies for addition facts within 20;
explore, develop and apply the commutative, associative and zero properties of addition;
add numbers without renaming within 99;
construct number sentences and number stories;
solve problems involving addition within 99.

1. **Add one to these numbers.**

 Start with the bigger number.

4 + 1 = ☐   6 + 1 = ☐   8 + 1 = ☐

1 + 15 = ☐   13 + 1 = ☐   1 + 17 = ☐

7 + 1 = ☐   1 + 1 = ☐   1 + 14 = ☐

2.

13	14	6	17	8	1	1	1	1	1
+ 1	+ 1	+ 1	+ 1	+ 1	+ 2	+9	+16	+ 11	+ 19
___	___	___	___	___	___	___	___	___	___

3. 11 + 1 + 0 = ☐   5 + 1 + 0 = ☐   0 + 13 + 1 = ☐

4. **True or false?** **or** ✗

5 + 1 = 6   ☑   20 + 1 = 20 ☐   1 + 13 = 13 ☐

15 + 0 + 0 = 20 ☐   2 + 1 + 10 = 13 ☐   12 + 1 = 20 ☐

5. **Draw a picture to show 9 + 8 = 17.**

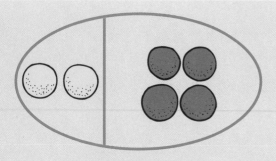

$$2 + 4 = 6 \qquad \text{and} \qquad 4 + 2 = 6$$

so $2 + 4 = 4 + 2$

When two numerals are the same, the answer is the same.

It doesn't matter which way you turn the sum.

It doesn't matter which number comes first.

1. **Try these.**

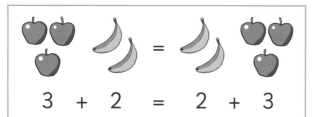

$3 + 2 = 2 + 3$ $4 + 1 = 1 + 4$

$5 + 12 = 12 + \boxed{}$ $15 + 4 = 4 + \boxed{}$ $11 + 8 = 8 + \boxed{}$

$7 + 13 = 13 + \boxed{}$ $4 + 13 = 13 + \boxed{}$ $12 + 7 = 7 + \boxed{}$

$13 + 5 = 5 + \boxed{}$ $6 + 11 = 11 + \boxed{}$ $3 + 12 = 12 + \boxed{}$

2. **Now try these.**

$6 + 13 = \boxed{} + 6$ $18 + 2 = \boxed{} + 18$ $4 + 15 = \boxed{} + 4$

$13 + 7 = \boxed{} + 13$ $9 + 11 = \boxed{} + 9$ $12 + 6 = \boxed{} + 12$

$7 + 12 = \boxed{} + 7$ $12 + 8 = \boxed{} + 12$ $14 + 5 = \boxed{} + 14$

Look Back – Double Trouble

 Do you remember your doubles and near doubles?

1. 1 + 1 = ☐   3 + 3 = ☐   6 + 6 = ☐   9 + 9 = ☐

    4 + 4 = ☐   8 + 8 = ☐   10 + 10 = ☐   7 + 7 = ☐

2. **Draw the missing spots on the butterfly's wings.**

 Double 2 is _____   Double 4 is _____   Double 6 is _____

 Double 8 is _____   Double 7 is _____   Double 9 is _____

 Double 5 is _____   Double 3 is _____   Double 1 is _____

3. **Write the missing doubles on the caterpillars.**

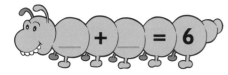 ___ + ___ = 6    ___ + ___ = 14   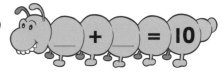 ___ + ___ = 10

 ___ + ___ = 20   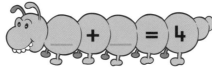 ___ + ___ = 4   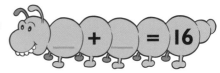 ___ + ___ = 16

4. **Use your doubles.**

   10 = 5 + 5   6 = ☐ + ☐   12 = ☐ + ☐

   8 = ☐ + ☐   4 = ☐ + ☐   16 = ☐ + ☐

   20 = ☐ + ☐   14 = ☐ + ☐   18 = ☐ + ☐

 Now how about learning the 'Doubles Rap'?

Near Doubles

Now try the doubles plus one. 'When numbers are neighbours, get the doubles to help.'

6 + 7 = ⬜ ?   The nearest double is **6 + 6** and I just add one more.

6 + 7 is the same as 6 + 6 + 1.

 Use doubles and near doubles to do these sums.

1. 4 + 5 = 4 + 4 + ☐1 = ☐   3 + 4 = 3 + 3 + ☐ = ☐

    5 + 6 = 5 + ☐ + ☐ = ☐   7 + 8 = 7 + ☐ + ☐ = ☐

    8 + 9 = 8 + ☐ + ☐ = ☐   9 + 10 = 9 + ☐ + ☐ = ☐

    10 + 11 = 10 + ☐ + ☐ = ☐   2 + 3 = 2 + ☐ + ☐ = ☐

2.
5	3	8	2	4	7	6	9	10
+ 5	+ 3	+ 8	+ 2	+ 4	+ 8	+ 7	+ 10	+11

3.
6	3	9	2	5	7	6	4	10
+ 6	+ 2	+ 8	+ 3	+ 4	+ 6	+ 5	+ 3	+ 9

Game Time
Play Doubles Hopscotch!

1. **Add the numbers in the balloons.**

 Add the doubles first.

4 + 4 + 5 = ☐   6 + 6 + 3 = ☐   3 + 3 + 6 = ☐

4 + 4 + 6 = ☐   7 + 7 + 4 = ☐   8 + 8 + 1 = ☐

9 + 9 + 2 = ☐   10 + 10 + 1 = ☐   5 + 6 + 6 = ☐

 Remember: 'When numbers are neighbours, get the doubles to help.'

2. **Try these.**

6 + 7 + 1 = ☐   2 + 3 + 0 = ☐   5 + 6 + 1 = ☐

4 + 5 + 3 = ☐   8 + 9 + 1 = ☐   10 + 11 + 0 = ☐

Now try the doubles less one.

6 + 5 = ☐?   The nearest double is **6 + 6** and then I take one away.

6 + 5 is the same as 6 + 6 −1

3. 4 + 3 = 4 + 4 − ☐1 = ☐ | 3 + 2 = 3 + 3 − ☐ = ☐

5 + 4 = 5 + ☐ − ☐ = ☐ | 7 + 6 = 7 + ☐ − ☐ = ☐

8 + 7 = 8 + ☐ − ☐ = ☐ | 9 + 8 = 9 + ☐ − ☐ = ☐

When you are adding three numbers, it doesn't matter which numbers you add first.

4 + 3 + 5 = 12   3 + 5 + 4 = 12   5 + 4 + 3 = 12

Use your ten boards to try these:

1.

5 + 7 + 3 = ☐

7 + 3 + 5 = ☐

3 + 5 + 7 = ☐

2.

2 + 6 + | 4 | = ☐

6 + 4 + ☐ = ☐

4 + 2 + ☐ = ☐

3.

3 + 4 + | 7 | = ☐

4 + 7 + ☐ = ☐

7 + 3 + ☐ = ☐

4.

4 + ☐ + ☐ = ☐

1 + ☐ + ☐ = ☐

9 + ☐ + ☐ = ☐

5.

5 + ☐ + ☐ = ☐

6 + ☐ + ☐ = ☐

4 + ☐ + ☐ = ☐

6.

6 + ☐ + ☐ = ☐

☐ + ☐ + ☐ = ☐

☐ + ☐ + ☐ = ☐

Puzzler

Jed is 2 years older than Jen. What ages could they be?
Here is one possibility. Can you think of some more?

Jed might be …	Jen might be …
6	4

Fact Families

Write two addition sentences and two subtraction sentences for these three numbers.

$6 + 1 = 7$

$1 + 6 = 7$

$7 - 1 = 6$

$7 - 6 = 1$

💡 When subtracting, the larger number is first.

1.

$3 + 2 = \boxed{}$

$2 + 3 = \boxed{}$

$5 - 3 = \boxed{}$

$5 - 2 = \boxed{}$

$6 + 3 = \boxed{}$

$3 + \boxed{} = \boxed{}$

$9 - 6 = \boxed{}$

$9 - \boxed{} = \boxed{}$

$7 + 5 = \boxed{}$

$5 + \boxed{} = \boxed{}$

$12 - 7 = \boxed{}$

$12 - \boxed{} = \boxed{}$

$9 + \boxed{} = \boxed{}$

$7 + \boxed{} = \boxed{}$

$16 - \boxed{} = \boxed{}$

$16 - \boxed{} = \boxed{}$

2.

___ + ___ = ___

___ + ___ = ___

___ − ___ = ___

___ − ___ = ___

___ + ___ = ___

___ + ___ = ___

___ − ___ = ___

___ − ___ = ___

___ + ___ = ___

___ + ___ = ___

___ − ___ = ___

___ − ___ = ___

___ + ___ = ___

___ + ___ = ___

___ − ___ = ___

___ − ___ = ___

3.

16	
13	3

18	
11	7

___ + ___ = ___

___ + ___ = ___

___ − ___ = ___

___ − ___ = ___

___ + ___ = ___

___ + ___ = ___

___ − ___ = ___

___ − ___ = ___

Puzzler

What is the missing number in the top red circle?
Hint: you may need to add.

Adding on Ten

0 1 2 3 4 5 6 7 8 9 10 11 12 13 14 15 16 17 18 19 20

 Do you notice anything when you add 10 to a one-digit number?

1. 10 + 3 = ☐   10 + 4 = ☐   10 + 6 = ☐   10 + 0 = ☐

2. **Now add 10 to these numbers.**

Does it matter if 10 is not the first number? _____

5 + 10 = ☐   8 + 10 = ☐   3 + 10 = ☐   2 + 10 = ☐

3.
10	10	10	10	10	10	10	10	9	4	7
+ 5	+ 7	+ 9	+ 4	+ 6	+ 1	+ 3	+ 8	+ 10	+ 10	+ 10
☐	☐	☐	☐	☐	☐	☐	☐	☐	☐	☐

4. 6 + ☐ = 16   4 + ☐ = 14   7 + ☐ = 17   9 + ☐ = 19

10 + ☐ = 15   10 + ☐ = 12   10 + ☐ = 18   10 + ☐ = 11

Do you remember the numbers that make 10?

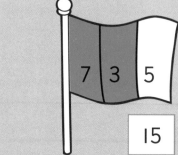

7 3 5

15

When you are adding, look for the numbers that make 10 to make you quicker.

7 + 3 = 10 so 7 + 3 + 5 = 15

5. **Colour the pairs that make 10. Add the numbers in the flags.**

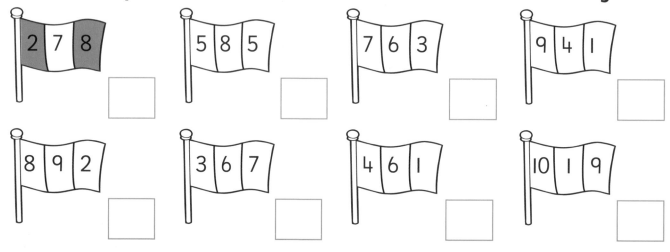

2 7 8   ☐

5 8 5   ☐

7 6 3   ☐

9 4 1   ☐

8 9 2   ☐

3 6 7   ☐

4 6 1   ☐

10 1 9   ☐

Count On

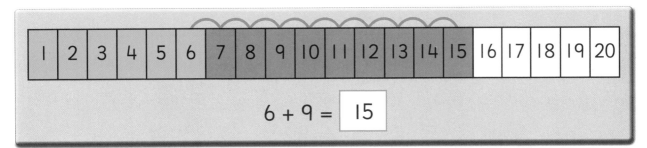

$$6 + 9 = \boxed{15}$$

1. **Count on, using the number strip.**

$7 + 4 = \boxed{\ .\ }$	$13 + 13 = \boxed{\ }$	$5 + 8 = \boxed{\ }$	$12 + 7 = \boxed{\ }$
$6 + 7 = \boxed{\ }$	$14 + 5 = \boxed{\ }$	$12 + 8 = \boxed{\ }$	$5 + 12 = \boxed{\ }$
$8 + 8 = \boxed{\ }$	$9 + 10 = \boxed{\ }$	$17 + 3 = \boxed{\ }$	$16 + 3 = \boxed{\ }$

2.

10	9	8	12	15	7	18	14	10	17	13
+ 10	+ 6	+ 9	+ 5	+ 5	+ 8	+ 2	+ 4	+ 9	+ 2	+ 6
☐	☐	☐	☐	☐	☐	☐	☐	☐	☐	☐

3. **Add the numbers in the apples. Circle the ones that add up to the number under the apple.**

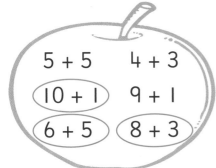

11

6 + 6   7 + 3
10 + 2   8 + 4
4 + 7   11 + 1

12

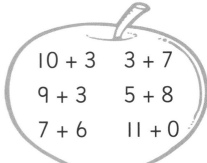

10 + 3   3 + 7
9 + 3   5 + 8
7 + 6   11 + 0

13

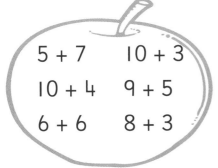

5 + 7   10 + 3
10 + 4   9 + 5
6 + 6   8 + 3

14

6 + 10   7 + 8
10 + 2   11 + 4
4 + 9   11 + 1

15

Puzzler

What number comes next?

1 → 2 → 4
8 → 16 → ? ☐

Adding Three Numbers

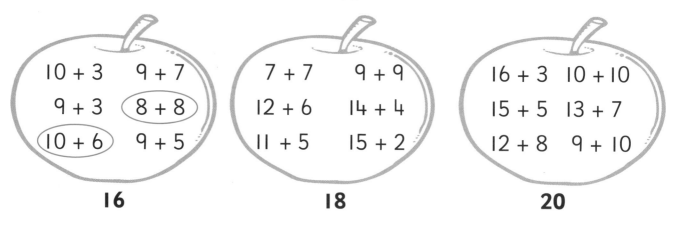

| 1 | 2 | 3 | 4 | 5 | 6 | 7 | 8 | 9 | 10 | 11 | 12 | 13 | 14 | 15 | 16 | 17 | 18 | 19 | 20 |

$$6 + 4 + 1 = \boxed{11}$$

1. $5 + 5 + 9 = \boxed{}$ $9 + 1 + 10 = \boxed{}$ $7 + 3 + 8 = \boxed{}$ $6 + 4 + 8 = \boxed{}$

   $4 + 6 + 10 = \boxed{}$ $8 + 2 + 9 = \boxed{}$ $3 + 8 + 3 = \boxed{}$ $6 + 6 + 3 = \boxed{}$

   $12 + 3 + 4 = \boxed{}$ $13 + 3 + 2 = \boxed{}$ $7 + 7 + 6 = \boxed{}$ $8 + 3 + 8 = \boxed{}$

2.
6	8	5	3	6	7	4	9	2	0
2	3	4	8	6	8	7	8	9	5
+ 6	+ 7	+ 6	+ 9	+ 6	+ 4	+ 6	+ 1	+ 6	+ 9

3. **Circle the correct sums in each apple.**

10 + 3	9 + 7		7 + 7	9 + 9		16 + 3	10 + 10
9 + 3	(8 + 8)		12 + 6	14 + 4		15 + 5	13 + 7
(10 + 6)	9 + 5		11 + 5	15 + 2		12 + 8	9 + 10

| **16** | **18** | **20** |

Recap

• I know how to add to a total of 20.   ○ ○ ○

• I can use different ways to find the answers
   – doubles, near doubles and finding number bonds to 10.   ○ ○ ○

3. Subtraction I

Look Back

1. **Cross out the correct number to get the answer.**

$9 - 3 =$ [6]

$11 - 4 =$ [ ]

$12 - 6 =$ [ ]

$8 - 2 =$ [ ]

$15 - 8 =$ [ ]

| 1 | 2 | 3 | 4 | 5 | 6 | 7 | 8 | 9 | 10 | 11 | 12 | 13 | 14 | 15 | 16 | 17 | 18 | 19 | 20 |

2.

$17 - 4 =$ [13] $16 - 6 =$ [ ] $11 - 8 =$ [ ] $19 - 7 =$ [ ]

$13 - 3 =$ [ ] $10 - 5 =$ [ ] $9 - 6 =$ [ ] $12 - 4 =$ [ ]

$16 - 8 =$ [ ] $11 - 5 =$ [ ] $8 - 1 =$ [ ] $17 - 9 =$ [ ]

$15 - 9 =$ [ ] $12 - 7 =$ [ ] $13 - 5 =$ [ ] $19 - 6 =$ [ ]

$20 - 8 =$ [ ] $14 - 2 =$ [ ] $17 - 4 =$ [ ] $16 - 7 =$ [ ]

$18 - 10 =$ [ ] $11 - 6 =$ [ ] $10 - 1 =$ [ ] $17 - 5 =$ [ ]

$12 - 3 =$ [ ] $13 - 8 =$ [ ] $14 - 8 =$ [ ] $20 - 10 =$ [ ]

$15 - 8 =$ [ ] $13 - 9 =$ [ ] $17 - 3 =$ [ ] $16 - 9 =$ [ ]

Strand: Number
Curriculum Objectives:
Develop an understanding of subtraction as deducting, as complementing and as difference;
develop and recall mental strategies for subtraction 0–20;
construct number sentences involving subtraction of whole numbers; solve problems involving subtraction;
estimate differences within 99;
subtract numbers without and with renaming within 99;
use the symbols +, –, =, <, >;
solve one-step and two-step problems involving subtraction.

More Subtraction

$11 - 7 = 4$

0 1 2 3 4 5 6 7 8 9 10 11 12 13 14 15 16 17 18 19 20

1. $20 - 7 =$ ☐ $11 - 4 =$ ☐ $14 - 3 =$ ☐ $10 - 7 =$ ☐

   $9 - 5 =$ ☐ $16 - 6 =$ ☐ $8 - 4 =$ ☐ $17 - 5 =$ ☐

   $12 - 9 =$ ☐ $18 - 5 =$ ☐ $7 - 2 =$ ☐ $15 - 9 =$ ☐

   $17 - 6 =$ ☐ $11 - 7 =$ ☐ $19 - 5 =$ ☐ $17 - 1 =$ ☐

   $20 - 3 =$ ☐ $6 - 4 =$ ☐ $8 - 7 =$ ☐ $13 - 6 =$ ☐

2.
15	7	13	16	19	11	15	16
− 0	− 6	− 2	− 4	− 2	− 3	− 4	− 9

3.
8	7	9	11	17	14	9	10
− 8	− 4	− 3	− 9	− 5	− 3	− 8	− 5

4.
20	17	16	18	11	14	17	13
− 8	− 4	− 7	− 10	− 6	− 8	− 4	− 8

5. **Draw a picture to show $18 - 7 = 11$.**

Subtraction Problems

Jane had 12 lollipops. She gave 4 to Julie. How many had she left?

1 2 3 4 5 6 7 8 9 10 11 12 13 14 15 16 17 18 19 20

12 − 4 = | 8 |

Write the subtraction sentence, then find the answer.

1. **Susie had 14 marbles. 3 rolled under her bed.
   How many had she left?**

   ☐ − ☐ = ☐

2. **Jamie had 19 toy soldiers. Benny the dog ate 7.
   How many had Jamie left?**

   ☐ − ☐ = ☐

3. **Lisa bought 18 jelly sweets. She gave 9 to her sister Laura.
   How many had she left?**

   ☐ − ☐ = ☐

4. **Leah picked 15 daisies. She gave 7
   to Lara. How many had she left?**

   ☐ − ☐ = ☐

5. **Ross collected 17 conkers in the park.
   He lost 8 of them on his way home.
   How many had he left?**

   ☐ − ☐ = ☐

6.

−	12	14	16
5			
4			
3			

−	18	19	20
8			
6			
4			

−	13	15	17
8			
7			
6			

Number Sentences

0 1 2 3 4 5 6 7 8 9 10 11 12 13 14 15 16 17 18 19 20

Make these number sentences correct.

You can use [+] or [−] or [=]   13 [+] 13 = 26

1. 15 [ ] 5 = 20   12 [ ] 4 = 8   14 + 4 [ ] 18

    10 [ ] 10 = 0   19 [ ] 11 = 8   16 − 12 [ ] 4

    17 [ ] 3 = 14   15 [ ] 12 = 3   20 [ ] 4 = 16

    18 [ ] 6 = 12   12 [ ] 7 = 19   13 [ ] 3 = 16

    5 [ ] 13 = 18   7 [ ] 11 = 18   16 [ ] 11 = 5

2. **Find the missing number.**

    12 − [ ] = 6   [ ] − 4 = 8   19 − [ ] = 12

    [ ] − 3 = 11   17 − [ ] = 10   [ ] − 2 = 16

    13 − [ ] = 7   [ ] − 5 = 13   20 − [ ] = 16

    [ ] − 7 = 8   10 − [ ] = 4   [ ] − 14 = 2

We can use other words to show we are taking away

subtract   minus   difference between

3. 11 minus 4 = [ ]   Take 3 from 15 = [ ]

    18 subtract 5 = [ ]   Take 6 from 17 = [ ]

    19 minus 10 = [ ]   Subtract 7 from 18 = [ ]

4. **What is the difference between 7 and 13?** [ ]

5. **What is the difference between 3 and 11?** [ ]

Number Problems

1. **John had 19 sheep. On Tuesday, he sold 8 sheep. How many has he left?**

   There are ☐ sheep left.

2. **Jasmine is making a jigsaw. The jigsaw should have 20 pieces but there are only 13 pieces in the box. How many more pieces does Jasmine need to find?**

   Jasmine needs to find ☐ jigsaw pieces.

3. **Grace collects dolls. There are 18 in a set. She has 7 dolls. How many more does she need to have a full set?**

   Grace needs to collect ☐ more dolls.

4. **This year Max got 9 Easter eggs. Dan got 14. What was the difference between the number of eggs they got?**

   The difference between the amount of eggs was ☐ .

5. **Mary is entering an art competition. She has 6 cards. To enter the competition, she needs 14 cards. How many more cards does she need to make?**

   Mary must make ☐ more cards.

Puzzler

In how many ways can you make 7 using the numbers 9, 6, 8, 5, 1 and + and −?

Recap

- I can find the difference between two numbers.
- I know different words for subtraction.
- I can solve problems using subtraction.

○ ○ ○
○ ○ ○
○ ○ ○

4. Addition and Subtraction to 20

Words that tell us to add +	Words that tell us to subtract –
add, plus, and, altogether, in total, more, sum of	take away, minus, how many fewer, how many left, difference between

Circle the correct sign. Write the number sentence.

1. There were 11 crabs on the beach. 7 were washed out to sea.

   How many crabs were left?

   + or –

   ☐ ☐ = ☐

2. Terry jumped over 9 waves. Dan jumped over 2 fewer than Terry. How many waves did Dan jump over?

   + or –

   ☐ ☐ = ☐

3. Kate saw 7 seagulls. Dad saw 6 seagulls.

   How many seagulls did they see in total?

   + or –

   ☐ ☐ = ☐

4. 14 children ate vanilla ice cream and 4 children ate chocolate ice cream.

   What is the difference between these numbers?

   + or –

   ☐ ☐ = ☐

5. There are 17 red flags at the beach. There are 14 blue flags in the shop.

   Take the number of blue flags from the number of red flags.

   + or –

   ☐ ☐ = ☐

6. Dad saw 13 sun umbrellas at the beach. Mum saw 5 umbrellas in the shop.

   What is 13 plus 5?

   + or –

   ☐ ☐ = ☐

Strand: Number
Curriculum Objectives:
Solve one-step problems involving addition or subtraction;
use the symbols +, – , =.

5. Counting and Numeration 1

Estimating and Counting

1.

Estimate		Estimate		Estimate	
Count		Count		Count	

Estimate		Estimate		Estimate	
Count		Count		Count	

2. **What numbers are missing?**

11	12		14	15
16	17			20
	14	15		
15			18	

15			17		19
14	15				18
		12	13		
16				19	

3. **Put these numbers in order, starting with the smallest.**

14, 6, 20, 16, 9

19, 11, 13, 7, 2

3, 6, 1, 18, 15

10, 17, 3, 16, 8

Strand: Number
Curriculum Objectives:
Count the number of objects in a set;
read, write and order numerals 0–20;
estimate the number of objects in a set 0–20.

6. Place Value 1

Tens and Units

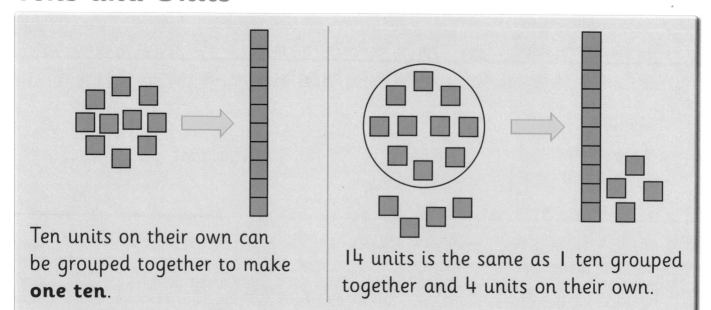

Ten units on their own can be grouped together to make **one ten**.

14 units is the same as 1 ten grouped together and 4 units on their own.

1. Group ten units into a ten and count how many are left. Circle the ten cubes you are using to make a ten.

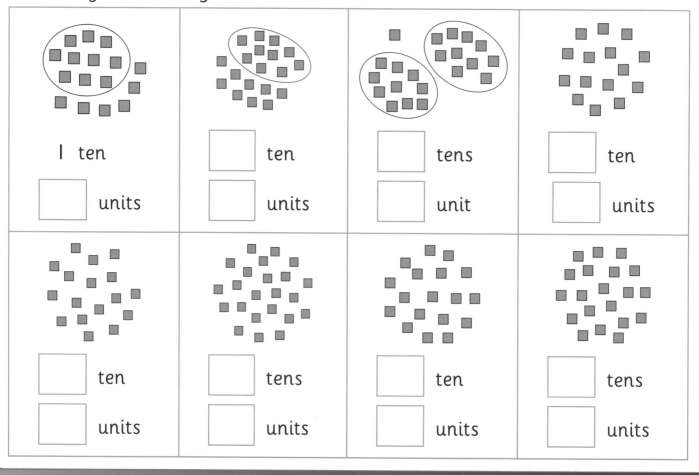

| 1 ten | ten | tens | ten |
| units | units | unit | units |

| ten | tens | ten | tens |
| units | units | units | units |

Strand: Number
Curriculum Objective:
Explore, identify and record place value 0–199.

Place Mat and Abacus!

Task: On your place mat and abacus, show the following numbers in tens and units.

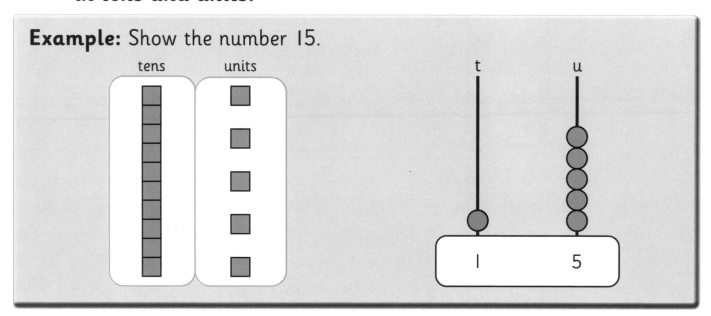

Example: Show the number 15.

1.

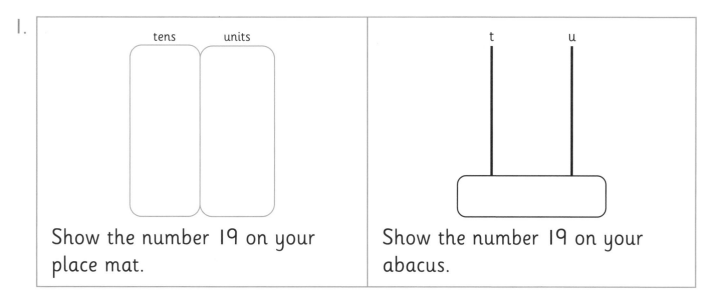

Show the number 19 on your place mat.

Show the number 19 on your abacus.

Show these numbers on the place mats.

2.

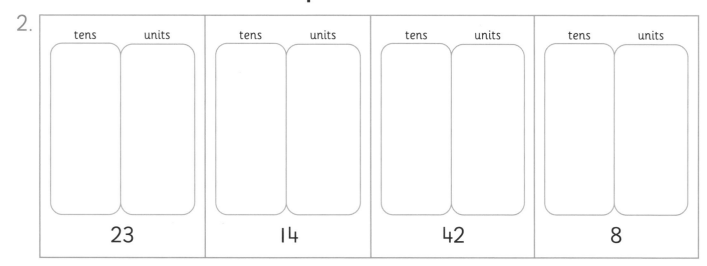

23   14   42   8

Show these numbers on the abacuses.

1.

t	u
2	8

t	u
3	1

t	u
6	4

t	u
2	7

2.

t	u
5	5

t	u
6	7

t	u
4	9

t	u
2	3

Figure it Out!

1. 16 = _____ ten and _____ units
   23 = _____ tens and _____ units
   19 = _____ ten and _____ units
   34 = _____ tens and _____ units
   11 = _____ ten and _____ unit
   25 = _____ tens and _____ units
   42 = _____ tens and _____ units
   55 = _____ tens and _____ units
   78 = _____ tens and _____ units

2. 99 = _____ tens and _____ units
   83 = _____ tens and _____ units
   65 = _____ tens pand _____ units
   79 = _____ tens and _____ units
   12 = _____ ten and _____ units
   47 = _____ tens and _____ units
   20 = _____ tens and _____ units
   51 = _____ tens and _____ unit
   10 = _____ ten and _____ units

Now try these:

3. 1 ten and 3 units = _____
   2 tens and 8 units = _____
   4 tens and 1 unit = _____
   6 tens and 6 units = _____
   7 tens and 3 units = _____
   9 tens and 1 unit = _____
   2 tens and 4 units = _____
   5 tens and 9 units = _____
   3 tens and 5 units = _____

4. 8 tens and 3 units = _____
   4 tens and 6 units = _____
   1 ten and 8 units = _____
   9 tens and 4 units = _____
   7 tens and 1 unit = _____
   4 tens and 9 units = _____
   2 tens and 6 units = _____
   3 tens and 4 units = _____
   0 tens and 8 units = _____

Puzzler

Look at these two numbers: 99 and 88.
How many tens and units in each number?
Now figure out how many tens and units
there are altogether in the two numbers.

Recap

• I know more about tens and units.
• I can show tens and units on a place mat.
• I can show tens and units on an abacus.

7. Data

Birthday Party Activities

bowling							
cinema							
art							

1. How many children want to go bowling? ☐

2. How many children want to go to the cinema? ☐

3. How many children want to have an art party? ☐

4. Which activity is the most popular? ☐

5. Which activity is the least popular? ☐

6. How many children prefer bowling to the cinema? ☐

7. How many children are going to the party altogether? ☐

8. How many children like bowling and art? ☐

9. How many more children like art than like bowling? ☐

10. How many fewer children like the cinema than like bowling? ☐

Strand: Data
Curriculum Objectives:
Sort and classify objects by two and three criteria;

represent, read and interpret simple tables and charts;
represent, read and interpret simple block graphs.

Seasonal Birthdays!

This is a block graph. A block graph uses blocks in place of pictures.

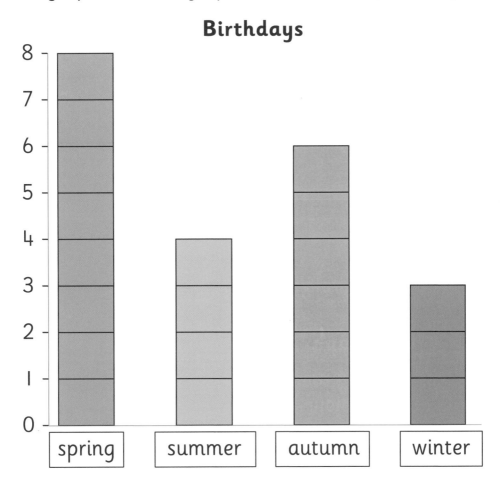

Birthdays

1. How many birthdays are there in spring? ☐

2. In which season are the most birthdays? _____

3. In which season are the fewest birthdays? _____

4. How many birthdays are shown on the graph? ☐

5. How many more birthdays are there in spring than in winter? ☐

6. How many fewer birthdays are there in summer than in autumn? ☐

7. How many birthdays are there in spring and autumn altogether? ☐

8. How many birthdays in summer, autumn and winter? ☐

A Trip to the Zoo

Second class went on a school tour to the zoo.

1. **The children saw:**

   ☐ elephants   ☐ giraffes   ☐ tigers   ☐ monkeys

2. **Let's make a block graph.**

   Colour one block for every animal.
   There are 3 giraffes, so colour 3 blocks.

   Remember:
   - A pictogram uses pictures.
   - A block graph uses blocks.

1. a) How many more monkeys are there than elephants?

   b) How many fewer tigers are there than giraffes?

   c) How many elephants and tigers are there altogether?

   d) How many more tigers are needed to equal the number of monkeys?

   e) How many fewer monkeys are needed to equal the number of giraffes?

True or false?

   f) There are less elephants than giraffes.

   g) There are 15 animals altogether.

   h) There are more monkeys than tigers.

Puzzler

A spider is at the bottom of a 30-metre drain pipe. Every day, the spider climbs up 5 metres. Every night, the spider is washed down 3 metres. How many days will it take for the spider to reach the top?

Recap

• I can sort and classify objects.
• I can make a graph based on information.
• I can answer questions based on the graph.

8. Addition 2

Adding on to Nine

We know it is easy to add on to ten.

10 + 3 = 13

Here is a little tip to help you add on to nine.

Nine wants to be 10, so it takes one from the next number.

   +

9 + 5

10 + 4 = 14

Now try these. Use your ten boards to help you.

1.   9 + 3

= 10 + ____

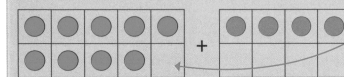

2.   9 + 7

= 10 + ____

3.   9 + 5

= 10 + ____

4.   9 + 8

= 10 + ____

5.   9 + 2

= 10 + ____

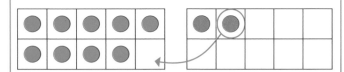

6.   9 + 6

= 10 + ____

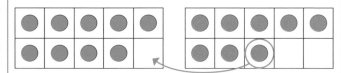

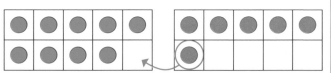

Strand: Number
Curriculum Objectives:
Add numbers without renaming within 99;
develop an understanding of addition by combining or
partitioning sets;

develop and recall mental strategies for addition facts within 20;
construct number sentences and number stories; solve
problems involving addition within 99.

Addition – Twenty and Beyond!

 Use 2 ten boards and 20 cubes to help you.

1. **Make 20.**

20 + [0] = 20   19 + [ ] = 20   18 + [ ] = 20

17 + [ ] = 20   16 + [ ] = 20   15 + [ ] = 20

14 + [ ] = 20   13 + [ ] = 20   12 + [ ] = 20

11 + [ ] = 20   10 + [ ] = 20   9 + [ ] = 20

0 1 2 3 4 5 6 7 8 9 10 11 12 13 14 15 16 17 18 19 20 21 22 23 24 25 26 27 28 29 30

2. **Add. Look for numbers that make 20 to help you.**

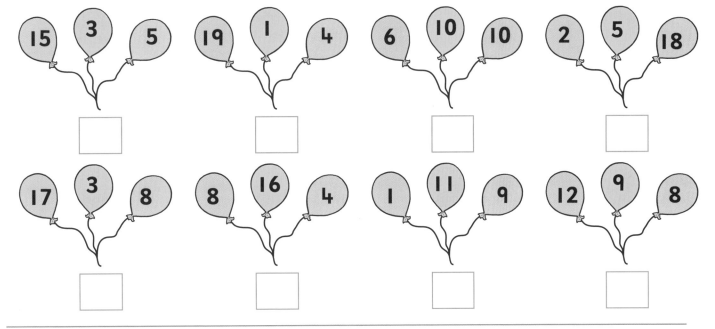

3. **Can you make 20 using three numbers?**

[ ] + [ ] + [ ] = 20   [ ] + [ ] + [ ] = 20

Puzzler

What are the next four numbers?

1, 3, 6, 10, 15, ____, ____, ____, ____

Do you remember the numbers that make 20?

17 2 3

22

Look for the numbers that make 20.

17 + 3 = 20   so   17 + 3 + 2 = 22

1. **Colour the pairs that make 20. Add.**

 12 7 8

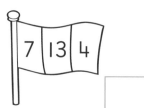 15 9 5

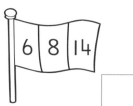 7 13 4

6 8 14

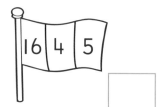 16 4 5

 3 5 15

 5 11 9

6 18 2

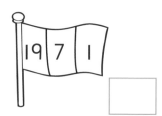 19 7 1

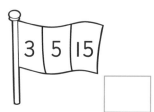 8 3 12

3 6 17

4 16 1

2. 2 + 12 + 8 = ☐   14 + 6 + 4 = ☐   15 + 8 + 5 = ☐

13 + 7 + 5 = ☐   9 + 18 + 2 = ☐   7 + 19 + 1 = ☐

10 + 4 + 10 = ☐   3 + 3 + 17 = ☐   11 + 7 + 9 = ☐

10 + 9 + 10 = ☐   13 + 9 + 7 = ☐   9 + 11 + 8 = ☐

Addition to 99

0 1 2 3 4 5 6 7 8 9 10 11 12 13 14 15 16 17 18 19 20

 Remember:
- Look for the numbers that make 10.
- Remember the doubles and near doubles.
- Start with the biggest number and count on.

1. $4 + 7 + 4 =$ ☐ $3 + 13 + 3 =$ ☐ $5 + 5 + 8 =$ ☐

   $2 + 12 + 7 =$ ☐ $2 + 10 + 7 =$ ☐ $3 + 6 + 9 =$ ☐

   $0 + 14 + 6 =$ ☐ $1 + 12 + 3 =$ ☐ $3 + 5 + 12 =$ ☐

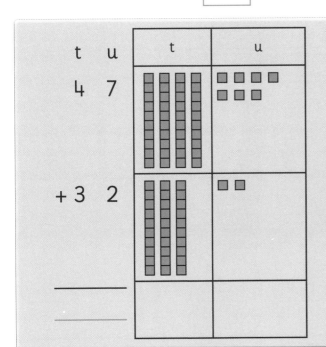

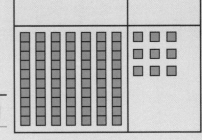

Remember to add the units first.

2.
t u	t u	t u	t u	t u	t u	t u	t u
1 7	2 4	1 6	2 2	3 6	1 8	2 8	1 6
+1 1	+1 2	+2 1	+1 5	+2 2	+2 1	+1 1	+2 2

3.
t u	t u	t u	t u	t u	t u	t u	t u
1 0	4 3	1	2 4	1 7	1 5	1 2	2 0
+3 9	+ 6	+4 4	+1 5	+3 2	+3 3	+3 6	+3 0

Help Hansel and Gretel Find their Way Home

1. **Add the numbers in the stones until you reach the house.**
   Start with the units.

t u	t u	t u	t u	t u	t u
1 5	1 6	2 5	1 8	3 3	2 2
+ 1 2	+ 1 3	+ 1 3	+ 2 1	+ 2 3	+ 3 5

t u	t u	t u	t u	t u	t u	t u	t u
1 8	3 2	4 8	1 6	4 1	2 2	1 0	8 3
+ 3 1	+ 2 3	+ 1 1	+ 5 2	+ 8	+ 1 4	+ 3 7	+ 6

t u	t u	t u	t u	t u	t u	t u	t u
4 1	3	2 4	1 5	1 5	1 2	2 0	4 3
+ 2 4	+ 5 4	+ 2 5	+ 3 3	+ 3 4	+ 3 6	+ 3 0	+ 3

t u	t u	t u	t u	t u	t u	t u	t u
3 6	1 5	7	3 4	4 4	2 5	3	2 5
+ 2 1	+ 3 4	+ 2 2	+ 2	+ 1 5	+ 5 1	+ 8 5	+ 5 0

t u	t u	t u	t u	t u	t u	t u	t u
4 5	2 1	2 3	1 6	1 2	1 2	2 9	4 3
+ 2 4	+ 5 4	+ 3 5	+ 8 3	+ 6 4	+ 3 6	+ 7 0	+ 3 2

t u	t u	t u	t u	t u	t u
4 5	2 4	3	7 0	3	4 2
+ 4 1	+ 5 4	+ 6 5	+ 3	+ 6 4	+ 3 7

Recap

- I know the number bonds to 20.
- I can add large numbers to 99 without renaming.

◯ ◯ ◯
◯ ◯ ◯

9. Check-up 1

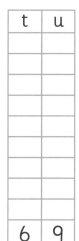

0 1 2 3 4 5 6 7 8 9 10 11 12 13 14 15 16 17 18 19 20

1. Add and subtract.

+	5	6	7
1			
2			
3			

+	10	12	14
2			
4			
6			

−	6	7	8
2			
3			
4			

−	13	14	15
1			
3			
5			

2. Write in the missing numbers.

| | 17 | | |

| | 9 | | 12 |

| 12 | | 14 | |

3. Draw the correct number on the notation board.

t	u
1	8

t	u
4	4

t	u
6	9

t	u
7	0

4. Write the number shown on each abacus.

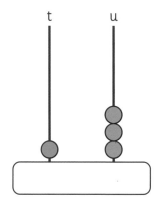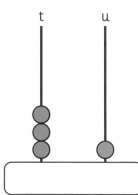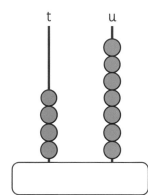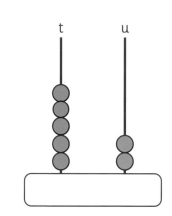

5.

```
  t u      t u      t u      t u      t u      t u      t u      t u      t u
  1 7      3 6      2 8      1 4      5 1      4 2      1 0      4 3      2 4
+ 2 2    + 1 3    + 3 1    + 2 2    +   6    + 5 5    + 3 9    + 1 3    + 5 3
_____    _____    _____    _____    _____    _____    _____    _____    _____
```

Curriculum Objective:
To revise concepts that were explored in units 2–8.

37

10. 2-D Shapes

 square   rectangle   triangle   circle   oval   semi-circle

Shapes can be found everywhere.
Shapes can have **straight** lines and **curved** lines.
All shapes have **sides**. Some shapes have **corners**.
Talk to your friend about these shapes.

Shape Detective

 Be a shape detective. Find 2-D shapes in the pictures below.

1. The coin is a _____ .

2. The map is a _____ .

3. The mirror is a _____ .

4. The traffic light sign is a _____ .

5. The frisbee is a _____ .

6. The window is a _____ .

Finished Early?

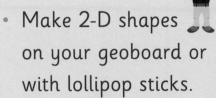

- Make 2-D shapes on your geoboard or with lollipop sticks.
- Discuss with your friend: how is a square different from a rectangle? How is a circle like an oval?

Strand: Shape and Space
Curriculum Objectives:
Sort, describe, compare and name 2-D shapes – square, rectangle, triangle, circle, semi-circle and oval;

identify and discuss the use of 2-D shapes in the environment;
construct and draw 2-D shapes;
combine and partition 2-D shapes;
identify half and quarter of shapes.

1. Match the shape to the word.

square   semi-circle   triangle   circle   oval   rectangle

2. Colour the shapes.

circle   **square**   **triangle**   oval   semi-circle   **rectangle**

3. How many of each shape can you see in the picture?

squares ☐   rectangles ☐   triangles ☐

circles ☐   semi-circles ☐   ovals ☐

4. Draw and colour these shapes.

yellow circle	black rectangle	blue square
red triangle	green oval	orange semi-circle

Puzzler

Lay out 12 lollipop sticks to make one big square with four smaller squares inside, like this picture.
Now move only **two** lollipop sticks to make seven squares.

1. **Explore 2-D shapes.**

corner ↙   ←— side

| rectangle | triangle | oval | circle | square | semi-circle |

Shape	Name	How many sides?	How many corners?	Does it have curved sides? ✓ or ✗	Does it have straight sides? ✓ or ✗

2. a) A _____ has four equal sides.

   b) A _____ has one curved side and one straight side.

   c) A _____ and an _____ have no corners.

   d) A _____ has two long sides and two short sides.

   e) A _____ and an _____ have only one side.

   f) Half a circle is a _____.

Recap

• I can recognise and name 2-D shapes – square, triangle, rectangle, circle, semi-circle and oval.
• I know how many sides and corners each shape has.

11. Angles

full turn	half turn right	half turn left	quarter turn right	quarter turn left
A to A	**A to C**	**A to C**	**A to B**	**A to D**

A full turn is called a **rotation**.

1. **Starting at the** *
   - Colour a **quarter turn** to the **right red**.
   - Colour a **quarter turn** to the **left blue**.
   - Colour a **half turn green**.

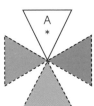 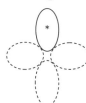 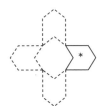 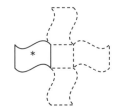

2. a) This is a . Colour in the picture that shows a half ($\frac{1}{2}$) turn.

   b) This is a . Ring the picture that shows a quarter ($\frac{1}{4}$) turn to the left.

Strand: Shape and Space
Curriculum Objectives:
Investigate objects that turn;
investigate full, half and quarter turns;
explore and recognise angles in the environment.

41

Angles

An **angle** is the space between two straight lines that meet.

Angle Activity
In pairs, make angles with your bodies, rulers, lollipop sticks, pencils, geostrips or straws. Find angles in the classroom.

1. Circle the smallest angle. Cross out X the largest angle.

2. **Draw an angle that is smaller and one that is larger than this first angle.**

	smaller angle	larger angle

Right Angles

A square has four square corners.

Sometimes angles make a square corner.   square corner

A square corner is called a **right angle**.

3. **Find objects that have right angles. Draw them below.**

1.	2.	3.	4.

4. **What is a right angle?** _____

A right angle is a square corner.

Angle Activity
Make right angles with pencils, lollipop sticks, rulers, clocks, etc.
Rotate right angles in $\frac{1}{4}$ and $\frac{1}{2}$ turns.

1. ✓ **right angles** ✗ **no right angles.**

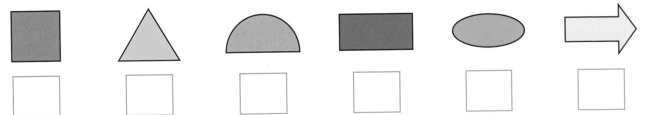

2. **Which of these crocodiles are making a right angle?**

   a) ✓ the crocodiles that are making right angles.

   b) Colour the crocodiles that are making
      an angle **smaller** than a right angle

   c) Circle the crocodiles that are making
      an angle **bigger** than a right angle.

 Puzzler

Draw a shape with **five right angles**.
You can also use other angles that are larger or smaller than a right angle.

Recap
• I can make $\frac{1}{4}$, $\frac{1}{2}$ and full turns or rotations.
• I know that an angle is the space between two straight lines that meet.
• I can recognise a right angle.

12. Subtraction 2

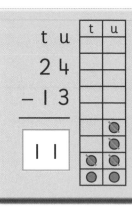

Remember to subtract the units first.

	t	u
2 4		
− 1 3		
1 1		

1.

	t	u
7 6		
− 3 4		

	t	u
8 8		
− 5 2		

	t	u
5 8		
− 3 4		

	t	u
9 7		
− 6 3		

	t	u
6 8		
− 4 7		

	t	u
4 9		
− 3 3		

2.

t u	t u	t u	t u	t u	t u	t u
9 6	8 5	7 9	2 9	8 6	9 5	7 7
− 5 3	− 5 5	− 3 5	− 1 6	− 3 4	− 5 1	− 4 2

3.

t u	t u	t u	t u	t u	t u	t u
4 8	7 9	9 5	9 0	8 2	5 4	7 9
− 3 8	− 5 3	− 6 2	− 5 0	− 2 1	− 4 4	− 5 3

Strand: Number
Curriculum Objectives:
Develop and recall mental strategies for subtraction;
solve problems involving subtraction;

estimate differences within 99;
subtract numbers without renaming within 99;
use the symbols +, −, =, <, >.

44

1. **Estimate by rounding first, then subtract.**

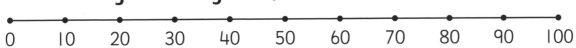

0   10   20   30   40   50   60   70   80   90   100

rounds to	rounds to	rounds to

Box 1

rounds to

t u		t u
4 6 ➡		5 0
− 2 3 ➡		− 2 0
23		**30**

Box 2

rounds to

t u		t u
5 8 ➡		60
− 3 1 ➡	−	30

Box 3

rounds to

t u		t u
6 5 ➡		70
− 4 0 ➡	−	40

Box 4

rounds to

t u		t u
3 8 ➡		
− 1 4 ➡	−	

Box 5

rounds to

t u		t u
7 7 ➡		
− 4 2 ➡	−	

Box 6

rounds to

t u		t u
9 2 ➡		
− 6 1 ➡	−	

Box 7

rounds to

t u		t u
8 6 ➡		
− 3 3 ➡	−	

Box 8

rounds to

t u		t u
6 5 ➡		
− 3 2 ➡	−	

Box 9

rounds to

t u		t u
5 7 ➡		
− 3 4 ➡	−	

Box 10

rounds to

t u		t u
5 9 ➡		
− 3 4 ➡	−	

Box 11

rounds to

t u		t u
8 3 ➡		
− 1 2 ➡	−	

Box 12

rounds to

t u		t u
6 9 ➡		
− 5 6 ➡	−	

Subtraction

0 1 2 3 4 5 6 7 8 9 10 11 12 13 14 15 16 17 18 19 20

1.
t u	t u	t u	t u	t u	t u
2 6	6 8	5 7	7 6	8 6	7 9
− 1 4	− 4 3	− 2 4	− 3 6	− 7 4	− 3 3
1 2					

2.
t u	t u	t u	t u	t u	t u
6 9	3 9	8 5	7 9	6 8	2 9
− 5 3	− 2 4	− 5 5	− 3 5	− 2 6	− 1 6

💡 Remember: Take away the units first.

3. 77 – 32 = ☐   65 – 23 = ☐   29 – 13 = ☐   75 – 41 = ☐

4. 60 – 20 = ☐   95 – 34 = ☐   78 – 62 = ☐   95 – 45 = ☐

5. 32 – 11 = ☐   56 – 22 = ☐   59 – 31 = ☐   69 – 28 = ☐

6. 87 – 44 = ☐   48 – 33 = ☐   86 – 53 = ☐   31 – 10 = ☐

Puzzler

Each line must have the numbers 1, 2, 3 and 4 going across, down and diagonally. Fill in the missing numbers.

3	4		1
1		4	3
	3		
2		3	

Recap

- I can subtract two-digit numbers. ○ ○ ○
- I know how to round numbers. ○ ○ ○
- I can use rounding to help me with subtraction. ○ ○ ○

13. Time 1

The Calendar

later day earlier date

> I week = 7 days
> A fortnight = 2 weeks or 14 days
> 12 months = 1 year

May						
Monday	Tuesday	Wednesday	Thursday	Friday	Saturday	Sunday
			1	2	3	
5		7	8	9	10	11
12	13			16	17	18
19		21	22	23		25
26		28	29		31	

1. **Fill in the missing dates in the calendar.**

2. **How many days are there in May?** ☐

3. **There are** ☐ **Thursdays in May.**

4. **The day before the 2nd of May is a** _____

5. **What day comes straight after the 23rd of May?** _____

6. **Megan played football on the** ☐ **nd of** _____

7. **She went to the dentist on the** ☐ **th of** _____

8. **What date is four days later than the 7th of May?** ☐ **th of May**

9. **What date is two days earlier than the 28th of May?** ☐ **th of May**

10. **What date is one week earlier than the 19th of May?** ☐ **th of May**

Finished Early?
Create a comic strip. Draw pictures to show what you do each day for a full week.

Strand: Measures
Curriculum Objectives:
Use the vocabulary of time to sequence events; read and record time using simple devices; read day, date and month using calendar and identify the season; discuss the passing of time: 24 hours in a day, 7 days in a week, number of days in the month.

Months and Seasons

Spring			Summer		
February 28/29	March 31	April 30	May 31	June 30	July 31
Autumn			Winter		
August 31	September 30	October 31	November 30	December 31	January 31

Seasons Challenge

How many days in:

Spring

Summer

Autumn

Winter

1. **There are** ___ **seasons in a year.**

2. **There are** ___ **months in a year.**

3. **Each season has** ___ **months.**

4. **January is in the season of** ___ .

5. **My birthday is in the season of** ___ .

6. **In which season is April Fool's Day?** ___

7. **In which season is Hallowe'en?** ___

8. **What season comes before winter?** ___

9. **What season comes after spring?** ___

10. **Colour the months of spring green, autumn brown, summer yellow and winter blue.**

Recap

- I know the days of the week, the months of the year and the seasons.
- I can read a calendar.

14. Length

1. **Estimate, then measure the length of your maths book.**

unit		estimate	measure
lollipop sticks			
cubes			
hand span			
pencils			

2. **Working in pairs, first estimate and then measure how many steps it takes you to walk the length of the classroom. Take turns to count your steps.**

estimate	number of steps

Did you and your partner get the same answer? _____

Why? _____

Strand: Measures
Curriculum Objectives:
Estimate, compare, measure and record length using non-standard units;

select and use appropriate non-standard measuring units/instruments;
estimate, measure and record length using metres and centimetres;
solve and complete practical tasks and problems involving length.

1. **Estimate and measure the length and width of your desk using the following non-standard units.**

My estimates

unit	length	width
lollipop sticks		
cubes		
pencil cases		
lunch boxes		

My exact answers

unit	length	width
lollipop sticks		
cubes		
pencil cases		
lunch boxes		

2. **Your teacher will choose one child to measure the width of the classroom by placing one foot in front of the other with no spaces in between. Now it's the teacher's turn to measure the width of the classroom in this way. Compare the difference in measurements. Why was there a difference?**

Using a Metre Stick

1. Estimate **if each object is** shorter than, **about** the same as, **or** longer than **a metre. Tick the box you think is correct.**

My estimates

	shorter than 1m	about 1m	longer than 1m
desk			
whiteboard			
length of the door			
school bag			
my height			
width of the window			

2. **Check using a metre strip.**

My exact answers

	shorter than 1m	about 1m	longer than 1m
desk			
whiteboard			
length of the door			
school bag			
my height			
width of the window			

3. **In your copy, draw all the objects that were:**

shorter than 1m	about the same as 1m	longer than 1m

1. **Estimate if the length of each object is** shorter than, **about** the same as, **or** longer than **half a metre. Tick the box you think is correct.**

My estimates

		shorter than $\frac{1}{2}$ m	about $\frac{1}{2}$ m	longer than $\frac{1}{2}$ m
desk				
school bag				
lunch box				
maths copy				
shoe				

2. **Use a $\frac{1}{2}$ metre string to see how accurate your estimates were.**

3. **We use centimetres to measure shorter objects. Estimate and measure the length of your book and your lunch box.**

a) book   Estimate = _____   Measurement = _____

b)  lunch box   Estimate = _____   Measurement = _____

4. **Now find these objects. Measure and write your answer.**

		measurement
pencil		_____ cm
lollipop stick		_____ cm
crayon		_____ cm

1. **Measure these lines:**

a) ⎯⎯⎯⎯⎯⎯ = [ ] cm

b) ⎯⎯⎯⎯⎯ [ ] cm

c) ⎯⎯⎯⎯⎯⎯⎯⎯ = [ ] cm

d) ⎯⎯⎯⎯⎯⎯⎯⎯

[ ] cm + [ ] cm = [ ] cm

2. **Draw the following lines in your copy:**

a) 7cm   b) 10cm   c) 3cm   d) 5cm

3. **Josh jumps 2 metres and then hops 5 metres. How many metres did Josh move altogether?** [ ] m

4. **Tom made a rocket that was 65cm long. Mary made a rocket that was 40cm long.**

a) Whose rocket was longer? [ ]   b) How much longer? [ ] cm

5. **What should Lisa use to measure the length of her table? Tick the correct answer.**

a) Lollipop sticks [ ]   b) A metre stick [ ]   c) Her feet [ ]

6. **What would you use to measure your finger?**

[ ] metres   [ ] centimetres

Recap

- I can estimate, measure, compare and record different lengths.
- I can choose appropriate measuring units.
- I know all about metres and centimetres.

○ ○ ○
○ ○ ○
○ ○ ○

15. Addition 3

Adding Numbers

1	2	3	4	5	6	7	8	9	10
11	12	13	14	15	16	17	18	19	20
21	22	23	24	25	26	27	28	29	30
31	32	33	34	35	36	37	38	39	40
41	42	43	44	45	46	47	48	49	50
51	52	53	54	55	56	57	58	59	60
61	62	63	64	65	66	67	68	69	70
71	72	73	74	75	76	77	78	79	80
81	82	83	84	85	86	87	88	89	90
91	92	93	94	95	96	97	98	99	100

$7 + 10 = \boxed{17}$ $35 + 10 = \boxed{45}$

Look at what happens when we add on 10.

1. **What is 10 more than 19?**

What is 10 more than 32?

What is 10 more than 28?

 Do you notice anything when you add 10 to a number?

2. $5 + 10 = \boxed{}$ $8 + 10 = \boxed{}$ $3 + 10 = \boxed{}$ $6 + 10 = \boxed{}$

$15 + 10 = \boxed{}$ $18 + 10 = \boxed{}$ $13 + 10 = \boxed{}$ $16 + 10 = \boxed{}$

$25 + 10 = \boxed{}$ $28 + 10 = \boxed{}$ $23 + 10 = \boxed{}$ $26 + 10 = \boxed{}$

$35 + 10 = \boxed{}$ $38 + 10 = \boxed{}$ $33 + 10 = \boxed{}$ $36 + 10 = \boxed{}$

3. $12 + 10 = \boxed{}$ $14 + 10 = \boxed{}$ $17 + 10 = \boxed{}$ $11 + 10 = \boxed{}$

$22 + 10 = \boxed{}$ $24 + 10 = \boxed{}$ $27 + 10 = \boxed{}$ $21 + 10 = \boxed{}$

$32 + 10 = \boxed{}$ $34 + 10 = \boxed{}$ $37 + 10 = \boxed{}$ $31 + 10 = \boxed{}$

$42 + 10 = \boxed{}$ $44 + 10 = \boxed{}$ $47 + 10 = \boxed{}$ $41 + 10 = \boxed{}$

 54

Strand: Number
Curriculum Objectives:
Develop an understanding of addition by combining or partitioning sets;
develop and recall mental strategies for addition facts within 20;

explore, develop and apply the commutative properties of addition;
add numbers without and with renaming within 99;
explore and discuss repeated addition and group counting;
construct number sentences and number stories;
solve problems involving addition within 99.

Remember:

$7 + 10 = 10 + 7$ $34 + 10 = 10 + 34$

You can turn the following sums around to make them easier to add.

1. $16 + 10 = \boxed{}$ $10 + 28 = \boxed{}$ $32 + 10 = \boxed{}$ $10 + 49 = \boxed{}$

     $10 + 69 = \boxed{}$ $10 + 71 = \boxed{}$ $10 + 80 = \boxed{}$ $25 + 10 = \boxed{}$

2.
$$\begin{array}{cccccccc} 10 & 10 & 10 & 10 & 10 & 10 & 10 & 10 \\ +45 & +29 & +49 & +62 & +84 & +56 & +31 & +83 \\ \hline \end{array}$$

Addition to 100 Use your 100-square to help you.

1	2	3	4	5	6	7	8	9	10
11	12	13	14	15	16	17	18	19	20
21	22	23	24	25	26	27	28	29	30
31	32	33	34	35	36	37	38	39	40
41	42	43	44	45	46	47	48	49	50
51	52	53	54	55	56	57	58	59	60
61	62	63	64	65	66	67	68	69	70
71	72	73	74	75	76	77	78	79	80
81	82	83	84	85	86	87	88	89	90
91	92	93	94	95	96	97	98	99	100

$25 + 5 = \boxed{30}$

3. $73 + 4 = \boxed{}$ $48 + 2 = \boxed{}$ $51 + 5 = \boxed{}$ $62 + 3 = \boxed{}$

4. $41 + 5 = \boxed{}$ $74 + 3 = \boxed{}$ $81 + 5 = \boxed{}$ $85 + 3 = \boxed{}$

5. $64 + 3 = \boxed{}$ $22 + 4 = \boxed{}$ $14 + 5 = \boxed{}$ $82 + 5 = \boxed{}$

6. $26 + 4 = \boxed{}$ $35 + 4 = \boxed{}$ $72 + 7 = \boxed{}$ $92 + 8 = \boxed{}$

7. $85 + 3 = \boxed{}$ $36 + 3 = \boxed{}$ $74 + 2 = \boxed{}$ $86 + 3 = \boxed{}$

Addition to 100

20 + 10 = 30

1	2	3	4	5	6	7	8	9	10
11	12	13	14	15	16	17	18	19	**20**
21	22	23	24	25	26	27	28	29	**30**
31	32	33	34	35	36	37	38	39	40
41	42	43	44	45	46	47	48	49	50
51	52	53	54	55	56	57	58	59	60
61	62	63	64	65	66	67	68	69	70
71	72	73	74	75	76	77	78	79	80
81	82	83	84	85	86	87	88	89	90
91	92	93	94	95	96	97	98	99	100

)+10

Adding on in Tens

40 + 20 = 60

1	2	3	4	5	6	7	8	9	10
11	12	13	14	15	16	17	18	19	20
21	22	23	24	25	26	27	28	29	30
31	32	33	34	35	36	37	38	39	**40**
41	42	43	44	45	46	47	48	49	**50**
51	52	53	54	55	56	57	58	59	**60**
61	62	63	64	65	66	67	68	69	70
71	72	73	74	75	76	77	78	79	80
81	82	83	84	85	86	87	88	89	90
91	92	93	94	95	96	97	98	99	100

)+10
)+10

Adding 20 is the same as adding 2 groups of 10 because 10+10 = 20

Adding 30 is the same as adding 3 groups of 10 because 10+10+10 = 30

1. 50 + 10 = ☐   50 + 20 = ☐   50 + 30 = ☐   50 + 40 = ☐

10 + 10 = ☐   10 + 20 = ☐   10 + 30 = ☐   10 + 40 = ☐

60 + 10 = ☐   60 + 20 = ☐   60 + 30 = ☐   60 + 40 = ☐

20 + 10 = ☐   20 + 20 = ☐   20 + 30 = ☐   20 + 40 = ☐

1	2	3	4	5	6	7	8	9	10
11	12	13	14	15	16	17	18	19	20
21	22	23	24	25	26	27	28	29	30
31	**32**	**33**	**34**	**35**	36	37	38	39	40
41	42	43	44	45	46	47	47	49	50
51	52	53	54	55	56	57	58	59	60
61	62	63	64	65	66	67	68	69	70
71	72	73	74	75	76	77	78	79	80
81	82	83	84	85	86	87	88	89	90
91	92	93	94	95	96	97	98	99	100

+10(

21 + 14 = 35

 Jump down in tens and move across in ones.

2. 24 + 12 = ☐   27 + 13 = ☐   25 + 23 = ☐   36 + 33 = ☐

33 + 46 = ☐   44 + 23 = ☐   55 + 24 = ☐   57 + 13 = ☐

80 + 18 = ☐   46 + 42 = ☐   62 + 36 = ☐   71 + 28 = ☐

Addition to 100 (Renaming)

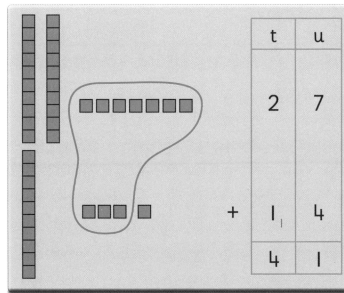

t	u
2	7
+ 1,	4
4	1

First, add all the units.

7 + 4 = 11

11 = 1 ten and 1 unit

Put 1 in the unit column and place 1 ten in the ten column.

Add all the tens to get your answer.

1.

t u	t u	t u	t u	t u	t u	t u
1 6	1 7	2 8	2 8	3 5	4 5	5 5
+, 8	+ 9	+ 8	+ 4	+ 9	+ 6	+ 8
2 4						

2.

t u	t u	t u	t u	t u	t u	t u
1 7	2 7	1 8	2 9	1 5	3 5	2 6
+1 8	+1 7	+3 6	+1 5	+3 7	+1 8	+2 9

Puzzler

What do you call a sleeping dinosaur?
Add to solve the riddle.

7	20	19	6	17	25	18	19	16	8
+15	+ 6	+ 8	+17	+17	+26	+ 5	+15	+12	+17

34	22	51	26	28	23	27	25
o	a	s	d	r	n	i	e

Addition to 100

1. **Help the spider get to its web by adding.**

0 1 2 3 4 5 6 7 8 9 10 11 12 13 14 15 16 17 18 19 20

	t u 1 5 +1 4	t u 1 6 +2 3	t u 1 5 +1 9	t u 2 5 +2 7	t u 1 6 +5 4	t u 6 3 +1 8
	2 9					
t u 3 9 +2 4	t u 5 7 +2 8	t u 1 1 +3 8	t u 4 7 +1 2	t u 6 9 +1 0	t u 3 9 +1 8	t u 7 6 + 6
t u 3 8 +3 4	t u 4 9 +1 9	t u 2 5 +4 9	t u 1 7 +6 7	t u 4 4 +3 5	t u 1 5 +6 2	t u 4 4 +1 4
t u 3 5 +4 3	t u 1 9 +2 7	t u 1 5 +3 8	t u 3 5 +1 5	t u 6 2 +1 7	t u 8 3 +1 4	t u 6 8 +2 8
t u 1 8 +1 9	t u 4 6 +2 7	t u 3 0 +3 8	t u 2 6 +1 9	t u 5 3 +2 6	t u 1 0 +5 9	t u 2 4 +3 5
t u 5 6 + 9	t u 4 +2 7	t u 2 +3 8	t u 2 6 + 7	t u 9 +2 4	t u 1 9 +5 9	

Finished Early?

Colour the squares where the answer has 9 units.

Puzzler

Can you put the numbers 3, 4, 5, 6 and 7 in the
boxes so that you get the same total when you
add the numbers in the row and in the column?
(Adding across or down.)

Hint: Put an odd number in the corner.

2. **Help the panda get to the bamboo leaves by adding.**

	t u	t u	t u	t u	t u	t u
	4 6	1 6	1 5	2 5	1 6	2 7
	1 2	1 2	2 5	5	2 1	3 7
	+ 2 7	+ 2 3	+ 1 9	+ 2 7	+ 5 4	+ 3 5
	8 5					

t u	t u	t u	t u	t u	t u	t u
3 9	5 7	1 1	4 7	6 9	3 9	7 6
2 0	1 2	3 0	1 6	4	3	1 4
+ 4	+ 8	+ 3 8	+ 1 2	+ 1 0	+ 1 4	+ 6

t u	t u	t u	t u	t u	t u	t u
3 5	1 6	1 5	3 5	6 2	5 3	2 8
3 3	2 3	2 2	6	1 0	6	2 1
+ 1 3	+ 2 6	+ 3 0	+ 1 5	+ 1 7	+ 1 4	+ 2 8

t u	t u	t u	t u	t u	t u	
1 5	1 3	3 0	2 6	5 3	1 0	
2	2 2	3 1	3 3	1 4	2 1	
+ 1 2	+ 4	+ 3 8	+ 1 9	+ 2 6	+ 5 8	

Finished Early?
Colour the squares where the answer is an even number.

R	**R**ead	Make sure you **read** the question – twice!
U	**U**nderstand	What is it asking you to do? Could you explain it to someone else?
C	**C**alculate	What calculation is needed? Have you estimated the answer?
S	**S**olve	What strategy are you going to use to solve the problem?
A	**A**nswer	Have you clearly shown your answer?
Ck	**Ch**ec**k**	Have you checked your calculation? Does it 'look' right?

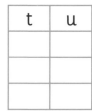
Remember: Rucsack!

Number Stories at the Cinema

1. **The shopkeeper sold 25 bags of salted popcorn. She sold 24 bags of unsalted popcorn.**

   The shopkeeper sold _____ bags of popcorn in total.

t	u

2. **18 ice creams were sold on Saturday. 31 ice creams were sold on Sunday.**

   How many ice creams were sold? _____

t	u

3. **13 children went to see a film on Monday. 14 went to see it on Tuesday and 12 went along on Wednesday.**

   _____ children went to see the film.

t	u

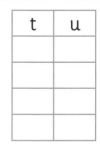

Recap

- I can add using a 100-square.
- I can count on and backwards in tens.
- I can add large numbers with and without renaming.
- I can solve simple maths problems.

16. 100-Square Subtraction

1	2	3	4	5	6	7	8	9	10
11	12	13	14	15	16	17	18	19	20
21	22	23	24	25	26	27	28	29	30
31	32	33	34	35	36	37	38	39	40
41	42	43	44	45	46	47	48	49	50
51	52	53	54	55	56	57	58	59	60
61	62	63	64	65	66	67	68	69	70
71	72	73	74	75	76	77	78	79	80
81	82	83	84	85	86	87	88	89	90
91	92	93	94	95	96	97	98	99	100

25 – 4 = 21

Put your finger on 25.
Jump back 4 places.
You land on 21.

| 21 | 22 | 23 | 24 | 25 |

1.

73 – 2 =   48 – 5 =   59 – 6 =   68 – 3 =

47 – 5 =   74 – 3 =   86 – 4 =   85 – 3 =

67 – 6 =   29 – 4 =   18 – 2 =   83 – 1 =

36 – 2 =   65 – 3 =   48 – 7 =   45 – 4 =

2. **Be careful – now you need to go back a row.**

23 – 4 =   35 – 7 =   72 – 7 =   92 – 8 =

85 – 8 =   36 – 9 =   54 – 9 =   66 – 8 =

25 – 5 =   22 – 5 =   41 – 5 =   34 – 4 =

27 – 9 =   83 – 5 =   73 – 4 =   82 – 5 =

Strand: Number
Curriculum Objective:
Develop an understanding of subtraction using the
100-square.

61

Counting Back in Tens

$$30 - 10 = 20 \qquad\qquad 60 - 20 = 40$$

1	2	3	4	5	6	7	8	9	10
11	12	13	14	15	16	17	18	19	20
21	22	23	24	25	26	27	28	29	30
31	32	33	34	35	36	37	38	39	40
41	42	43	44	45	46	47	48	49	50
51	52	53	54	55	56	57	58	59	60
61	62	63	64	65	66	67	68	69	70
71	72	73	74	75	76	77	78	79	80
81	82	83	84	85	86	87	88	89	90
91	92	93	94	95	96	97	98	99	100

$\}-10$

1	2	3	4	5	6	7	8	9	10
11	12	13	14	15	16	17	18	19	20
21	22	23	24	25	26	27	28	29	30
31	32	33	34	35	36	37	38	39	40
41	42	43	44	45	46	47	48	49	50
51	52	53	54	55	56	57	58	59	60
61	62	63	64	65	66	67	68	69	70
71	72	73	74	75	76	77	78	79	80
81	82	83	84	85	86	87	88	89	90
91	92	93	94	95	96	97	98	99	100

$\}-10$
$\}-10$

Subtracting 20 is the same as subtracting two groups of 10.

1. $80 - 10 = \boxed{}$ $\quad 50 - 20 = \boxed{}$ $\quad 70 - 30 = \boxed{}$ $\quad 60 - 40 = \boxed{}$

   $50 - 10 = \boxed{}$ $\quad 70 - 20 = \boxed{}$ $\quad 90 - 30 = \boxed{}$ $\quad 40 - 20 = \boxed{}$

   $60 - 10 = \boxed{}$ $\quad 90 - 20 = \boxed{}$ $\quad 50 - 30 = \boxed{}$ $\quad 80 - 40 = \boxed{}$

1	2	3	4	5	6	7	8	9	10
11	12	13	14	15	16	17	18	19	20
21	22	23	24	25	26	27	28	29	30
31	32	33	34	35	36	37	38	39	40
41	42	43	44	45	46	47	48	49	50
51	52	53	54	55	56	57	58	59	60
61	62	63	64	65	66	67	68	69	70
71	72	73	74	75	76	77	78	79	80
81	82	83	84	85	86	87	88	89	90
91	92	93	94	95	96	97	98	99	100

$35 - 14 = ?$

$14 = 10$ and 4, so take away 10 first, then take away 4

$35 - 10 - 4 = 21$

 Jump back in tens and then move back in ones.

2. $24 - 11 = \boxed{}$ $\quad 27 - 12 = \boxed{}$ $\quad 66 - 13 = \boxed{}$ $\quad 62 - 31 = \boxed{}$

   $32 - 22 = \boxed{}$ $\quad 36 - 23 = \boxed{}$ $\quad 73 - 21 = \boxed{}$ $\quad 53 - 24 = \boxed{}$

   $44 - 33 = \boxed{}$ $\quad 48 - 32 = \boxed{}$ $\quad 55 - 17 = \boxed{}$ $\quad 82 - 16 = \boxed{}$

   $79 - 28 = \boxed{}$ $\quad 80 - 18 = \boxed{}$ $\quad 41 - 32 = \boxed{}$ $\quad 100 - 43 = \boxed{}$

17. Counting and Numeration 2

Read, Write and Order Numerals to 100

1. **Write the missing numbers behind the stars.**

1	2	☆	4	5	6	7	8	9	10
11	12	13	14	15	16	☆	18	19	20
21	☆	23	24	25	26	27	28	29	30
31	32	33	☆	35	36	37	38	39	40
41	42	43	44	☆	46	47	48	49	50
☆	52	53	54	55	56	57	57	59	60
61	62	63	64	65	☆	67	68	69	70
71	72	73	74	75	76	77	☆	79	80
81	82	83	84	85	86	87	88	☆	90
91	92	93	94	95	96	97	98	99	★

☆	3	☆	
☆		★	
☆		☆	
☆		☆	
☆		★	

2. **Write the missing numbers.**

17   27   44   87

3.

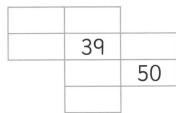

39   50   41   52   68   77

4. **Write the number on the flag.**

forty-nine = 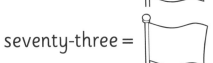 eighty-two =   sixty-five =

ninety-four =   twenty-one =   seventy-three =

one hundred =   thirty-six =   fifty-seven =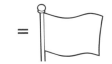

Strand: Number
Curriculum Objective:
Read, write and order numerals 0-99.

63

Rounding to the Nearest Ten

1. Look at the 100-square and round these numbers to the nearest 10.

> 💡 Remember: if the number ends in a 5, round it **up** to the nearest 10.

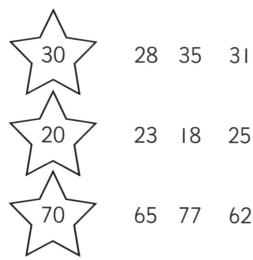

1	2	3	4	5	6	7	8	9	10
11	12	13	14	15	16	17	18	19	20
21	22	23	24	25	26	27	28	29	30
31	32	33	34	35	36	37	38	39	40
41	42	43	44	45	46	47	48	49	50
51	52	53	54	55	56	57	58	59	60
61	62	63	64	65	66	67	68	69	70
71	72	73	74	75	76	77	78	79	80
81	82	83	84	85	86	87	88	89	90
91	92	93	94	95	96	97	98	99	100

27 → ☐   42 → ☐

51 → ☐   39 → ☐

68 → ☐   14 → ☐

15 → ☐   80 → ☐

96 → ☐   33 → ☐

2. Circle the number nearest to the number in the star.

⭐ 30   28   35   31   ⭐ 40   39   43   36

⭐ 20   23   18   25   ⭐ 80   76   88   83

⭐ 70   65   77   62   ⭐ 90   87   92   86

3. Match each bee to its nearest hive.

45   39   57   52   61   43   54

40   50   60

Rounding to the Nearest Ten

1. **Round these numbers to the nearest 10.**

   13 rounds to ☐   26 rounds to ☐   34 rounds to ☐

   45 rounds to ☐   98 rounds to ☐   62 rounds to ☐

   89 rounds to ☐   77 rounds to ☐   15 rounds to ☐

2. **Round the numbers to the nearest ten to get an estimate. Then do the sum.**

estimate	add
18 + 21 ☐ 20 + ☐ 20 = ☐ 40	18 + 2 1 ———
27 + 32 ☐ + ☐ = ☐	2 7 + 3 2 ———
33 + 14 ☐ + ☐ = ☐	3 3 + 1 4 ———
44 + 36 ☐ + ☐ = ☐	4 4 + 3 6 ———
55 + 18 ☐ + ☐ = ☐	5 5 + 1 8 ———

3. **Match each sum to the correct estimate.**

11 + 16	40
23 + 21	20
8 + 9	30
39 + 19	60
27 + 21	80
46 + 36	90
59 + 15	50

4. **Maria planted 26 plants in her garden in autumn and 13 in spring. How many did she plant altogether? Circle the best estimate.**

   10   20   30   40   50

5. **Farmer Green had 27 lambs in one field and 24 in another field. How many lambs did he have altogether? Circle the best estimate.**

   20   30   40   50   60

Recap

• I can read, write and order numbers to 100.

• I can round numbers to the nearest 10.

1. **Draw 2 triangles in this box.**

2. **Name the shapes.**

 _____    _____

3. **The angles in a square** **are called** _____ **angles.**

4. **Subtract:**				5. **Add:**			
t u	t u	t u	t u	t u	t u	t u	t u
6 7	4 9	5 8	9 7	4 8	2 9	6 5	3 9
− 2 2	− 2 5	− 2 3	− 5 0	+ 2 7	+ 3 3	+ 2 5	+ 4 7
___	___	___	___	___	___	___	___

6. **Round these numbers to the nearest ten.**

   32 → [ ]   47 → [ ]   21 → [ ]   75 → [ ]   88 → [ ]

7. **There are** [ ] **hours in a day.   There are** [ ] **days in a week.**

   There are [ ] **months in a year.**

8. **Name something shorter than I metre.** _____

9. **Measure this line:** ——————— [ ] **cm**

10. **Write the missing numerals.**

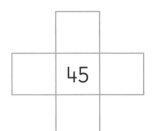   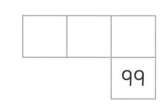

45   87   99   66

19. Comparing and Ordering

1. Colour the cloud that has the bigger number.

a) 11 15   b) 9 13   c) 17 21

d) 6 16   e) 19 14   f) 5 12

g) 22 35   h) 49 55   i) 63 21

2. Colour the cloud that has the smaller number.

a) 13 17   b) 7 11   c) 12 21

d) 25 16   e) 18 16   f) 51 14

g) 10 19   h) 30 13   i) 22 42

Strand: Number
Curriculum Objectives:
Compare equivalent and non-equivalent sets;
use the language of ordinal number.

67

Think of the symbol as a hungry mouth and think of the numbers as yummy sweets...

Which stash of sweets would you eat?

1. **Use the correct symbol** | < or > |.

11 ☐ 17	21 ☐ 11	25 ☐ 16
29 ☐ 16	17 ☐ 43	12 ☐ 55
18 ☐ 19	33 ☐ 15	44 ☐ 12
16 ☐ 41	35 ☐ 57	47 ☐ 59
13 ☐ 19	25 ☐ 44	31 ☐ 17
20 ☐ 25	42 ☐ 38	57 ☐ 75

greater than	equals	less than
>	=	<

2. **Now use all three symbols** | <, = or > |.

10 ☐ 20	32 ☐ 19	16 ☐ 16
25 ☐ 36	18 ☐ 43	14 ☐ 31
18 ☐ 18	33 ☐ 33	29 ☐ 19
14 ☐ 41	23 ☐ 53	47 ☐ 47
22 ☐ 22	55 ☐ 35	76 ☐ 67
12 ☐ 11	50 ☐ 5	10 ☐ 10

True or False?

	true or false?
bananas (12) < bananas (10)	false
cars (10) < cars (17)	
tennis balls (13) > tennis balls (14)	
pencils (12) = pencils (12)	
apples (19) > apples (18)	
pencil cases (11) > pencil cases (11)	
planes (18) < planes (22)	

Work it Out!

Put the correct symbol in each box <, = or > .

1.
15 ☐ 14 + 3

11 ☐ 20 – 5

7 ☐ 15 – 0

10 ☐ 70 – 10

2.
15 ☐ 19 – 2

25 ☐ 40 + 10

16 + 8 ☐ 22

16 + 4 ☐ 19

3.
9 + 9 ☐ 14 – 8

50 + 10 ☐ 35 + 12

3 + 8 ☐ 10 – 8

4.
0 + 9 ☐ 9 + 1

18 – 6 ☐ 9 + 8

12 – 10 ☐ 5 + 8

5.
54 + 10 ☐ 34 + 30

32 + 20 ☐ 28 + 20

6.
10 + 80 ☐ 75 – 10

20 + 8 ☐ 8 + 4

7.
greater than	less than	equal to

72 is _____ _____ 87

62 is _____ _____ 51

32 is _____ _____ 32

Puzzler

2 ducks in front of 2 ducks, 2 ducks behind
2 ducks, 2 ducks between 2 ducks.

How many ducks altogether?

Ordinal Numbers

The Calendar
This is Kate's calendar of events for the month of March.
Answer the questions below.

March						
Sunday	Monday	Tuesday	Wednesday	Thursday	Friday	Saturday
			1	2	3	4
5	6	7	8	9	10	11
12	13	14	15	16	17	18
19	20	21	22	23	24	25
26	27	28	29	30	31	

1. **What day is the first of March?** _____

2. **What day is the last day in March?** _____

3. **What date is the first Sunday in March?** [ ]

4. **What date is the last Saturday in March?** [ ]

5. **On how many days does Kate have art?** [ ]

6. **On what dates does Kate have basketball?** [ ] **and** [ ]

7. **What date is one week after the 3rd of March?** [ ]

8. **On what date does Kate have a birthday party?** [ ]

9. **What does Kate do on the third Monday in March?** _____

10. **The 23rd is the** _____ **Thursday in March.**

11. **How many days are there in March?** [ ]

Treasure Hunt Time

Jack and his friends are having a treasure hunt for Jack's birthday. When they get the clues, they must fill in the answers on the answer sheet and discover the word that the letters make. There are 10 clues to find.

The first clue they find is the letter T.

The second last clue is the letter O.

The third clue is the letter L.

The third last clue is the letter I.

The last clue is the letter N.

The clue after T is the letter E.

The fourth clue is the letter E.

The clue after the fourth clue is V.

The sixth clue is the same as the third last clue.

The seventh clue is the letter S.

1st	2nd	3rd	4th	5th	6th	7th	8th	9th	10th

Draw a picture of the word in the box below.

 Puzzler – Make Your Own!

Pick a word. Give your friend clues to figure it out.

 Puzzler

Look at a calendar of the year. There are 12 months in a year. Does every month have the same number of 2s?

Recap

- I can compare sets based on more and less.
- I can use symbols for greater than, less than and equal to.
- I can order numbers from 1st to 10th.

20. Spatial Awareness

1. **Discuss the positions of the animals in the jungle.**

left ←
right →
above
below
beside
between
under
lower than
higher than
next to

parrot

snake

frog

tiger

crocodile

butterfly

monkey

spider

ant

a) The ant is to the _____ of the tiger.

b) The frog is to the _____ of the spider.

c) The monkey is _____ the butterfly.

d) The parrot is _____ the crocodile.

e) The snake is _____ _____ the monkey.

f) The tiger is _____ the snake.

2. **Draw each toy in the correct box.**
   - The robot is **above** the doll.
   - The train is **below** the teddy.
   - The car is between the train and doll.
   - The drum is to the **left** of the robot.

Recap
- I can give and follow directions. ◯ ◯ ◯

Strand: Shape and Space
Curriculum Objectives:
Explore, discuss, develop and use the vocabulary of spatial relations;
give and follow directions in classrooms and school settings, including
turning directions using half and quarter turns.

21. Symmetry

Shapes that can fold in half so that one half folds exactly on the other half are **symmetrical**.

The fold line is the **line of symmetry**. Sometimes shapes have more than one line of symmetry.

These shapes are symmetrical: These shapes are **not** symmetrical:

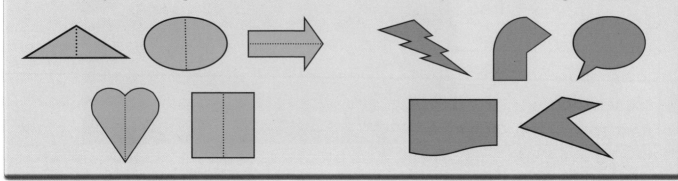

1. ✓ **the symmetrical shapes.** ✗ **the shapes that are** not **symmetrical.**

2. **Draw in a line of symmetry in each picture. Colour the shapes that have more than one line of symmetry.**

Finished Early?

In your copy, draw your own symmetrical shape.

Strand: Shape and Space
Curriculum Objective:
Identify line symmetry in shapes and in the environment.

Symmetry

1. Complete these symmetrical patterns.

a)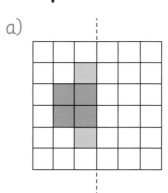

b)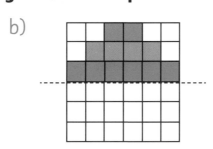

Puzzler

Use 10 cubes.
In three moves,
change the pattern
from a) to b).

a)   b)

2. In how many ways can you fold these shapes symmetrically?

The fold lines are the **lines of symmetry**.
Draw the lines of symmetry on your shapes.

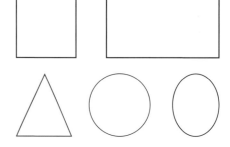

3. True or False?

a) A square has 4 lines of symmetry. _____

b) A rectangle has 3 lines of symmetry. _____

c) The triangle has only one line of symmetry. _____

d) A circle has more than 4 lines of symmetry. _____

4. Is the dotted line a line of symmetry? ✓ or ✗

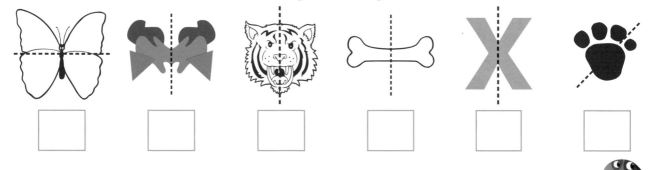

Recap

- I know symmetry is when a shape can be folded
  in half so that one half folds exactly on the other.
- The fold line is the line of symmetry.
- Some shapes have several lines of symmetry.

22. Subtraction 3

Tens and Units

Can you remember the rule for subtracting tens and units?

- First subtract the **units**.
- Then subtract the **tens**.

Now try this one . . .   54 – 7 =

You can't take away 7 from 4. What do you do now?

t	u
5	4
	7

RENAME!

t	u
⁴5̶	¹4
	7
4	7

Now try these:

1.
t	u
3	3
	7

t	u
²3̶	¹3
	7

2.
t	u
4	4
	8

t	u
	8

3.
t	u
3	6
	9

t	u
	9

4.
t	u
6	3
	5

t	u
	5

5.
t	u
5	2
	5

t	u
	5

6.
t	u
7	1
	7

t	u
	7

Strand: Number
Curriculum Objectives:
Develop an understanding of subtraction as deducting, as complementing and as difference;
develop and recall mental strategies for subtraction 0–20;
construct number sentences involving subtraction of whole numbers;
solve problems involving subtraction;
estimate differences within 99;
subtract numbers without and with renaming within 99;
solve one-step and two-step problems involving subtraction.

Subtraction

1.

t	u
6	0
−		6

→

t	u
−		6

2.

t	u
5	7
−		8

→

t	u
−		8

3.

t	u
2	2
−		5

→

t	u
−		5

4.

t	u
4	1
−		6

→

t	u
−		6

5.

t	u
3	5
−		7

→

t	u
−		7

6.

t	u
4	5
−		8

→

t	u
−		8

7.

t	u
2	8
−		9

→

t	u
−		9

8.

t	u
1	5
−		8

→

t	u
−		8

9.

t	u
4	1
−		2

→

t	u
−		2

10.

t	u
3	0
−		3

→

t	u
−		3

11.

t	u
6	8
−		9

→

t	u
−		9

12.

t	u
3	5
−		8

→

t	u
−		8

13.

t	u
2	0
−		6

→

t	u
−		6

14.

t	u
1	4
−		9

→

t	u
−		9

Subtraction

This time try renaming with two digits!

1.

t	u
4	6
– 1	9

➡

t	u
³4̶	¹6
– 1	9
2	7

2.

t	u
7	3
– 2	5

➡

t	u
– 2	5

3.

t	u
7	2
– 1	5

➡

t	u
– 1	5

4.

t	u
8	1
– 2	7

➡

t	u
– 2	7

5.

t	u
6	0
– 3	6

➡

t	u
– 3	6

6.

t	u
5	1
– 4	8

➡

t	u
– 4	8

7.

t	u
3	2
– 2	5

➡

t	u
– 2	5

8.

t	u
5	1
– 3	6

➡

t	u
– 3	6

9.

t	u
6	3
– 1	7

➡

t	u
–	

10.

t	u
5	7
– 2	9

➡

t	u
–	

Subtraction – Renaming

```
      t  u
     4⁄5 ¹3
    – 2  8
    ─────
      2  5
```

When you rename . . .
write it above the numbers.

1.
```
      t  u
    ²3⁄ ¹1
   – 1  9
   ──────
```
```
      t  u
      4  7
   – 2  8
   ──────
```
```
      t  u
      6  3
   – 4  4
   ──────
```
```
      t  u
      5  1
   – 3  5
   ──────
```
```
      t  u
      7  2
   – 5  6
   ──────
```

2.
```
      t  u
      4  2
   – 1  8
   ──────
```
```
      t  u
      5  3
   – 3  4
   ──────
```
```
      t  u
      3  3
   – 1  5
   ──────
```
```
      t  u
      6  6
   – 2  8
   ──────
```
```
      t  u
      8  1
   – 4  7
   ──────
```

On your own . . .

3.
```
      t  u
    ²3⁄ ¹1
   – 1  8
   ──────
      1  3
```
```
      t  u
    ²3⁄ ¹7
   – 2  9
   ──────
```
```
      t  u
      5  3
   – 4  5
   ──────
```
```
      t  u
      4  1
   – 3  6
   ──────
```
```
      t  u
      6  2
   – 5  7
   ──────
```

4.
```
      t  u
      2  1
   –    9
   ──────
```
```
      t  u
      3  4
   – 1  9
   ──────
```
```
      t  u
      7  7
   – 5  9
   ──────
```
```
      t  u
      4  0
   – 2  5
   ──────
```
```
      t  u
      8  5
   – 5  8
   ──────
```

Subtraction

1.
t u	t u	t u	t u	t u
6 4	4 0	7 5	3 6	9 2
− 1 8	− 1 6	− 2 7	− 9	− 6 6

2.
t u	t u	t u	t u	t u
5 4	6 0	3 8	6 3	4 6
− 2 7	− 2 1	− 1 9	− 5 4	− 3 8

3. **Find Emma's teddy. When you find the answer to each sum, cross out the teddy with this number on it.**

t u	t u	t u	t u	t u
5 0	3 2	8 2	4 4	6 7
− 3 6	− 1 3	− 2 9	− 1 7	− 3 8

53 14 27 25 19 29

4.
t u	t u	t u	t u	t u
4 2	2 0	4 6	5 5	7 4
− 3 7	− 1 2	− 8	− 1 6	− 2 9

Mixed Subtraction

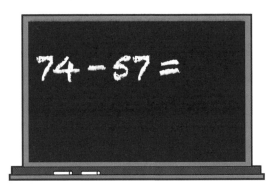

74 – 57 =

 Remember: You don't always need to rename.

1.
t u	t u	t u	t u	t u	t u	t u
7 4	9 0	7 3	4 8	8 1	5 0	8 8
– 5 7	– 6 0	– 2 6	– 1 2	– 6 5	– 9	– 4 7

2.
t u	t u	t u	t u	t u	t u	t u
9 8	5 9	7 6	7 2	3 2	5 3	6 0
– 6 1	– 1	– 5 9	– 5 6	– 1 1	– 2 3	– 2 7

3.
t u	t u	t u	t u	t u	t u	t u
9 4	6 7	4 6	2 4	5 4	6 1	7 2
– 3 0	– 5 2	– 2 3	– 4	– 1 0	– 4 6	– 5 8

4.
t u	t u	t u	t u	t u	t u	t u
4 5	6 5	3 9	6 3	8 4	5 0	3 4
– 3 5	– 5 0	– 3 3	– 1 7	– 5 1	– 3 9	– 1 6

5. **Now try these in your copy.**

61 – 28 = ☐   51 – 24 = ☐   65 – 28 = ☐

80 – 62 = ☐   37 – 19 = ☐   43 – 18 = ☐

81 – 43 = ☐   77 – 46 = ☐   68 – 59 = ☐

69 – 52 = ☐   92 – 78 = ☐   41 – 27 = ☐

Mixed Subtraction

1.
t u	t u	t u	t u	t u	t u	t u
8 8	8 5	4 8	6 6	5 7	4 5	7 1
− 5 1	− 6 6	− 3 7	− 5 1	− 3 0	− 2 1	− 5 9

2.
t u	t u	t u	t u	t u	t u	t u
9 7	4 2	8 4	8 9	7 9	5 7	4 0
− 1 5	− 3	− 2 3	− 5 3	− 6 1	− 2 3	− 1 7

3.
t u	t u	t u	t u	t u	t u	t u
5 3	4 6	8 7	6 2	4 6	8 7	8 5
− 4 1	− 3 6	− 6 7	− 2 9	− 2 5	− 3 9	− 5 9

4. **Crack the code.**
What do you get from nervous cows?

k	h	l	e	a	i
t u	t u	t u	t u	t u	t u
7 8	5 1	2 5	9 7	6 0	8 2
− 3 2	− 2 8	− 8	− 4 2	− 4 4	− 6 9

s	m
t u	t u
7 8	4 3
− 1 6	− 1 6

27	13	17	46

62	23	16	46	55	62

> < =

1. Finish these number sentences by filling in the missing symbol. Use < or > or =.

a) 19 − 3 ☐ 7 − 5

b) 13 − 11 ☐ 18 − 16

c) 18 − 10 ☐ 19 − 11

d) 14 − 12 ☐ 17 − 10

e) 13 − 6 ☐ 14 − 9

f) 18 − 14 ☐ 16 − 12

g) 20 − 9 ☐ 17 − 11

h) 12 − 8 ☐ 17 − 6

i) 18 − 6 ☐ 15 − 3

j) 14 − 4 ☐ 13 − 3

k) 19 − 13 ☐ 18 − 14

l) 16 − 11 ☐ 17 − 5

m) 17 − 11 ☐ 14 − 3

n) 18 − 12 ☐ 13 − 4

o) 15 − 5 ☐ 20 − 10

p) 20 − 13 ☐ 18 − 11

Puzzler

John is 12 years old. He has two sisters. Mary is three times as old as Josie. If John is seven years older than Josie, how old is Mary?

Recap

- I can subtract numbers without and with renaming.
- I know how to use these symbols: >, <, =.

○○○
○○○

23. Fractions

1. **Colour half of each shape.**

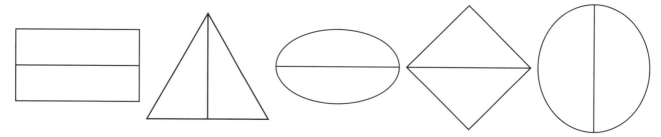

2. **Colour the shapes that show two halves.**

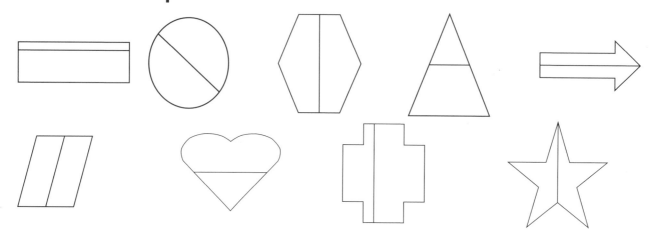

3. **Colour half of the apples.**

$\frac{1}{2}$ of 8 = ☐	$\frac{1}{2}$ of 12 = ☐	$\frac{1}{2}$ of 10 = ☐
$\frac{1}{2}$ of 14 = ☐	$\frac{1}{2}$ of 16 = ☐	$\frac{1}{2}$ of 20 = ☐

Strand: Number
Curriculum Objective:
Establish and identify halves and quarters of sets to 20.

Monkey Heaven!

1.

3 is half of **6**	🍌🍌🍌 🍌🍌🍌
2 is half of ___	🍌🍌 🍌🍌
6 is half of ___	🍌🍌🍌🍌🍌🍌 🍌🍌🍌🍌🍌🍌
5 is half of ___	🍌🍌🍌🍌🍌 🍌🍌🍌🍌🍌
10 is half of ___	🍌🍌🍌🍌🍌🍌🍌🍌🍌🍌 🍌🍌🍌🍌🍌🍌🍌🍌🍌🍌

2. **Now colour half the bananas on your own . . .**

🍌🍌🍌🍌🍌🍌🍌🍌🍌🍌🍌🍌🍌🍌🍌🍌🍌🍌	$\frac{1}{2}$ of 18 is ___
🍌🍌🍌🍌🍌🍌🍌🍌🍌🍌🍌🍌🍌🍌	$\frac{1}{2}$ of 14 is ___
🍌🍌🍌🍌🍌🍌🍌🍌	$\frac{1}{2}$ of 8 is ___
🍌🍌	$\frac{1}{2}$ of 2 is ___
🍌🍌🍌🍌🍌🍌🍌🍌🍌🍌🍌🍌🍌🍌🍌🍌	$\frac{1}{2}$ of 16 is ___

3. **Answer these questions.**

a) Lucy bought 12 sweets. She ate half of them.
   How many had she left? ☐

b) Jack's mam bought some marbles. She gave half of them to Jack.
   Jack got 10. How many did Jack's mam buy? ☐

c) There were 18 children in second class. Half of them were boys.
   How many were boys? ☐

d) Jane had 20 pages in her book. She read half of them. How many
   pages did she read? ☐

e) There were 14 elephants in the zoo. The zoo keeper gave water to half
   of them. How many got water? ☐

4. **In your copy . . .**
   Think of some shapes. Draw a half of each shape. Ask your partner to
   draw the other half.

Quarters

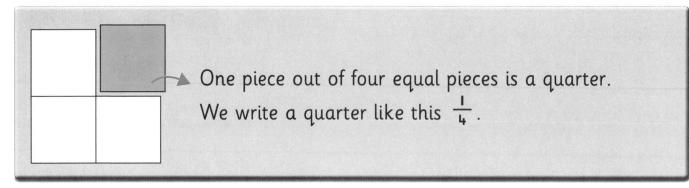

One piece out of four equal pieces is a quarter.
We write a quarter like this $\frac{1}{4}$.

1. **Find the quarter. Colour the quarter.**

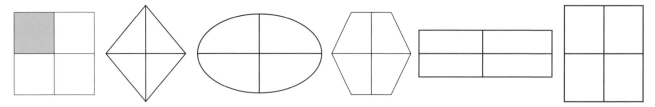

2. **Find a quarter of each set. Colour one quarter ($\frac{1}{4}$).**

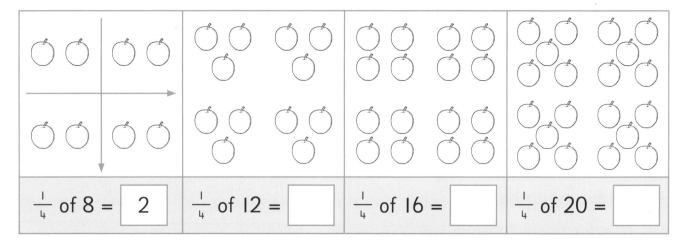

$\frac{1}{4}$ of 8 = 2 $\frac{1}{4}$ of 12 = ☐ $\frac{1}{4}$ of 16 = ☐ $\frac{1}{4}$ of 20 = ☐

3. **How do you find a quarter? Find half and then half again.**

$\frac{1}{2}$ of 8 = 4 ➡ $\frac{1}{2}$ of 4 = 2   so $\frac{1}{4}$ of 8 = 2

$\frac{1}{2}$ of 4 = ☐ ➡ $\frac{1}{2}$ of 2 = ◯   so $\frac{1}{4}$ of 4 = ☐

$\frac{1}{2}$ of 20 = ☐ ➡ $\frac{1}{2}$ of 10 = ◯   so $\frac{1}{4}$ of 20 = ☐

$\frac{1}{2}$ of 12 = ☐ ➡ $\frac{1}{2}$ of 6 = ◯   so $\frac{1}{4}$ of 12 = ☐

Problems!

1. **There were 14 children on the football team. Half of them lived near the pitch. How many lived near the pitch?** ☐

2. **Anna's granny bought 20 sweets. She gave half of them to Anna.**

   a) How many did she keep for herself? ☐

   b) Anna decided to give half of her sweets to her friend Jane. How many did Jane get? ☐

   c) What fraction of the sweets did Jane get? ☐

3. **Mammy bought a pizza for dinner. She cut the pizza into four equal slices. Each slice had 4 pieces of pepperoni.**

   a) How many pieces of pepperoni were on the whole pizza? ☐

   b) How many pieces of pepperoni were on half the pizza? ☐

4. $\frac{1}{2}$ of 20 = ☐ $\frac{1}{2}$ of 16 = ☐ $\frac{1}{2}$ of 24 = ☐

   $\frac{1}{4}$ of 12 = ☐ $\frac{1}{4}$ of 8 = ☐ $\frac{1}{4}$ of 20 = ☐

Puzzler
Five children are sitting at the blue group. If each child high fives the others at their table twice, how many high fives were there altogether? ☐

Recap
- I can find half and a quarter of shapes.
- I know that half of a half is a quarter.
- I can solve problems containing fractions.

24. Weight

1. **Estimate and then check using your balance.**

use your cubes	object	estimate	weight in cubes
	HOMEWORK DIARY		

Strand: Measures
Curriculum Objectives:
Estimate, compare, measure and record weight using non-standard units;
select and use appropriate non-standard measuring units and instruments;

estimate, measure and record weight using kilogram, half kilogram and quarter kilogram and solve simple problems; explore and discuss instances when objects or substances that weigh 1kg vary greatly in size.

Weight

1. Choose the non-standard measuring unit you are going to use.
2. Estimate how many of this unit it will take to balance the object.
3. Balance the object and record your results.
   You can use the following units:

| cubes | lollipop sticks | pencils |

this is what you must balance	Which unit are you going to use? Draw a picture or write the word	estimate how many you need	weight
Maths			

Weight

A bag of sugar weighs 1 kilogram.
1 kilogram is written as 1 kg.

1. **Estimate and then use a balance to check your answer.**

object	estimate		
	heavier than 1 kg	about the same as 1 kg	lighter than 1 kg
HOMEWORK DIARY			
Maths			

Weight

Some objects are lighter than a kilogram.

This tub of margarine weighs $\frac{1}{2}$ kg

I need 2 tubs to make a kilogram $\frac{1}{2}$ kg + $\frac{1}{2}$ kg = 1kg

1. **Estimate if these objects are lighter than, about the same as or heavier than $\frac{1}{2}$ kg.**

object	estimate		
	heavier than $\frac{1}{2}$ kg	about the same as $\frac{1}{2}$ kg	lighter than $\frac{1}{2}$ kg

This block of butter weighs $\frac{1}{4}$ kg

I need 4 blocks to make a kilogram $\frac{1}{4}$ kg + $\frac{1}{4}$ kg + $\frac{1}{4}$ kg + $\frac{1}{4}$ kg = 1kg

2. **Estimate if these objects are lighter than, about the same as or heavier than $\frac{1}{4}$ kg .**

object	estimate		
	heavier than $\frac{1}{4}$ kg	about the same as $\frac{1}{4}$ kg	lighter than $\frac{1}{4}$ kg

Problems!

1. **Michael's school bag weighs 4 kg. Susan's bag weighs twice as much as Michael's bag. How much do both bags weigh altogether?**

2. **A farmer bought a 34 kg bag of feed for his horses. The horses ate 17kg of it. How much is left in the bag?**

3. **When Granny is making a cake, she makes a mistake and puts too much flour in the bowl. She only needs $\frac{1}{4}$ kg of flour but has $\frac{1}{2}$ kg in the bowl. How much flour does she need to take out?**

4. **The Kelly family are going on holiday. Mam's bag weighs 18kg; Dad's bag weighs 15kg and Michael's bag weighs 19kg. What is the total weight of the three bags?**

5. **Mammy bought $\frac{1}{2}$ kg of tomatoes. Daddy bought two tubs of butter each weighing $\frac{1}{4}$ kg. Whose shopping is heavier?** _____

Puzzler

A bunch of bananas weighs 2kg. A bag of tomatoes weighs 1kg. They are both put into a shopping basket that weighs 6kg. What is the total weight of the bananas, tomatoes and shopping basket?

Recap

- I can estimate and record the weight of an object.
- I can choose an appropriate measuring unit.
- I know all about kilograms, $\frac{1}{2}$ kg and $\frac{1}{4}$ kg.

92   Weight

25. Time 2

What Can You Do in One Minute?

 Use a minute timer to help with this page.

How far can you count?	How many boys' names can you say?	How many fruit and vegetables can you name?
Can you say the alphabet?	Can you count in twos?	How many pets can you name?
Can you write the days of the week?	How many times can you write your name?	What else could you do? Make up a task for your friend.

Strand: Measures
Curriculum Objectives:
Use the vocabulary of time to sequence events;
read and record time using simple devices;

read time in hours, half-hours and quarter-hours on a 12-hour analogue clock;
read time in hours and half-hours on a digital clock;
discuss the passing of time: 24 hours in a day, 7 days in a week, numbers of days in the month.

Time

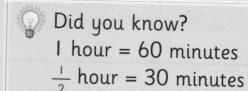
Did you know?
1 hour = 60 minutes
$\frac{1}{2}$ hour = 30 minutes

4 o'clock – the long hand points to 12

Half past 7 – the long hand points to 6

1. What time is it?

4 o'clock

_____ _____ _____ _____

_____ _____ _____ _____ _____

2. Show the correct time.

3 o'clock $\frac{1}{2}$ past 2 $\frac{1}{2}$ past 10   11 o'clock $\frac{1}{2}$ past 4

5 o'clock $\frac{1}{2}$ past 9 $\frac{1}{2}$ past 1   6 o'clock   half past three

94   Time 2

A Quarter Past the Hour

When the long hand points to **3** it is **a quarter ($\frac{1}{4}$) past** an hour

It is $\frac{1}{4}$ **past** 7

1. **What time is it?**

$\frac{1}{4}$ past ☐ $\frac{1}{4}$ past ☐ $\frac{1}{4}$ past ☐   ☐ past ☐   ☐ past ☐

2. **Make the clock say:**

$\frac{1}{4}$ past 7 $\frac{1}{4}$ past 1 $\frac{1}{4}$ past 11 $\frac{1}{4}$ past 5   quarter past 2

Puzzler

If a snail travels 1m in $\frac{1}{4}$ of an hour, how far will it travel in 1 hour? ☐ m

How far will it travel in 2 hours? ☐ m

Finished Early? Draw these clocks in your copy.

a) a quarter past 12   b) $\frac{1}{4}$ past 3   c) $\frac{1}{4}$ past 6   d) $\frac{1}{4}$ past 8

e) $\frac{1}{4}$ past 1   f) $\frac{1}{4}$ past 4   g) $\frac{1}{4}$ past 11   h) $\frac{1}{4}$ past 5

A Quarter to the Hour

  When the long hand is at **9** it is $\frac{1}{4}$ **to an hour**  It is $\frac{1}{4}$ **to** 8

1. **What time is it?**

$\frac{1}{4}$ to ☐

$\frac{1}{4}$ to ☐

$\frac{1}{4}$ to ☐

$\frac{1}{4}$ to ☐

2. **Make the clock say:**

$\frac{1}{4}$ to 12 $\frac{1}{4}$ to 5 $\frac{1}{4}$ to 10 $\frac{1}{4}$ to 1 $\frac{1}{4}$ to 6

3. **Tell your partner how to make the clock say:** a) $\frac{1}{4}$ to 11 b) $\frac{1}{4}$ to 6

Finished Early? Draw these clocks in your copy.

a) $\frac{1}{4}$ to 5 b) quarter to 9 c) quarter to 4 d) $\frac{1}{4}$ past 2 e) $\frac{1}{4}$ to 7

Digital Time

How do we write digital time?
Hint: We write the **hour** first.

 4:00

 4:30

1. **Write the digital time.**

3:00
_____   _____   _____   _____   _____

_____   _____   _____   _____   _____

_____   _____   _____   _____   _____

2. **Write the digital time.**

six thirty   = 6:30   four o'clock   = ☐   nine o'clock   = ☐

$\frac{1}{2}$ past 4 = ☐   half past ten = ☐   three thirty   = ☐

one o'clock = ☐   five thirty   = ☐ $\frac{1}{2}$ past seven = ☐

Digital Time

I. **Make the clocks say:**

5:00

7:00

11:00

2:30

10:30

3:30

12:30

1:00

4:30

9:00

8:30

2:00

6:00

5:30

12:30

3:00

Gym Classes for Kids

$\frac{1}{2}$ past 3	Judo
4 o'clock	Hip hop dance
$\frac{1}{2}$ past 4	Boxing for girls
5 o'clock	Gymnastics
$\frac{1}{2}$ past 5	Irish dancing
$\frac{1}{4}$ to 6	Karate
$\frac{1}{4}$ past 6	Boxing for boys
7 o'clock	Soccer skills

1. **What time does boxing for boys start?** _____
2. **What time does boxing for girls finish?** _____
3. **How long does karate last?** _____
4. **Which class starts at 5:30?** _____
5. a) What is your favourite activity? _____
   b) At what time does it begin? _____
   c) At what time does it finish? _____
   d) How long does the class last? _____

Recap

- I can read the time on an analogue clock and a digital clock.
- I can make a clock say o'clock, half past, a quarter past and a quarter to an hour.
- I can read a simple timetable.

○ ○ ○

○ ○ ○
○ ○ ○

26. Check-up 3

1. **Write the correct sign: >, < or =.**

18 ☐ 43   25 ☐ 11   11 + 7 ☐ 20 – 2   8 + 6 ☐ 7 + 9

2. **Colour the symmetrical letters and shapes.**

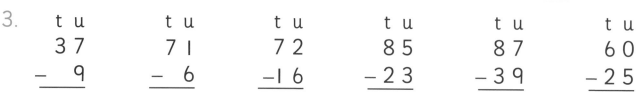

3.
```
  t u        t u        t u        t u        t u        t u
  3 7        7 1        7 2        8 5        8 7        6 0
–   9      –   6      – 1 6      – 2 3      – 3 9      – 2 5
─────      ─────      ─────      ─────      ─────      ─────
```

4. **What fraction is coloured?**

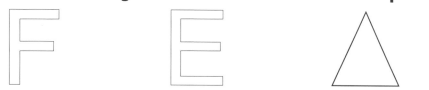

a) ☐

b) ☐

5. a) $\frac{1}{2}$ of 14 = ☐   b) $\frac{1}{4}$ of 20 = ☐

c) 9 is half of ☐   d) 2 is a quarter of ☐

6. ☐ **weighs more than a kg.**

7. **What time is it?**

_____   _____   _____   _____

8. **Write in digital time:**

3 o'clock = ☐ $\frac{1}{2}$ past 5 = ☐

Curriculum Objective:
To revise concepts that were explored in units 19–25.

27. Algebra – Extending and Using Patterns

Counting in Twos

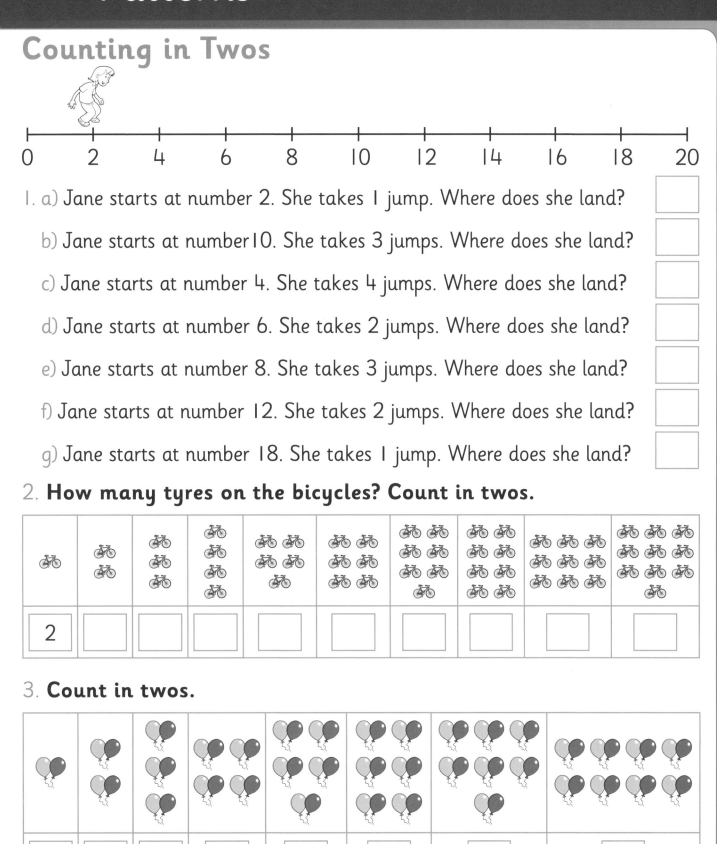

```
 +----+----+----+----+----+----+----+----+----+----+
 0    2    4    6    8    10   12   14   16   18   20
```

1. a) Jane starts at number 2. She takes 1 jump. Where does she land? ☐

   b) Jane starts at number 10. She takes 3 jumps. Where does she land? ☐

   c) Jane starts at number 4. She takes 4 jumps. Where does she land? ☐

   d) Jane starts at number 6. She takes 2 jumps. Where does she land? ☐

   e) Jane starts at number 8. She takes 3 jumps. Where does she land? ☐

   f) Jane starts at number 12. She takes 2 jumps. Where does she land? ☐

   g) Jane starts at number 18. She takes 1 jump. Where does she land? ☐

2. **How many tyres on the bicycles? Count in twos.**

2	☐	☐	☐	☐	☐	☐	☐	☐	☐

3. **Count in twos.**

☐	☐	☐	☐	☐	☐	☐	☐

Strand: Algebra
Curriculum Objectives:
Recognise patterns and predict subsequent numbers;
explore and use patterns in addition facts;
understand the use of a frame to show the presence of an
unknown number.

Counting in Fours

1. **Draw 4 spots on each dog.**

a) How many spots on 3 dogs? ☐

b) How many spots on 6 dogs? ☐

c) How many spots on 8 dogs? ☐

d) How many spots on 5 dogs? ☐

e) How many spots on 4 dogs? ☐

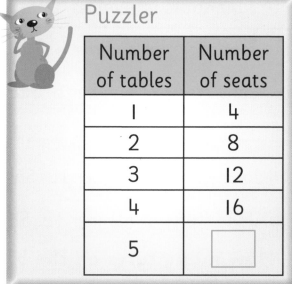

Puzzler

Number of tables	Number of seats
1	4
2	8
3	12
4	16
5	☐

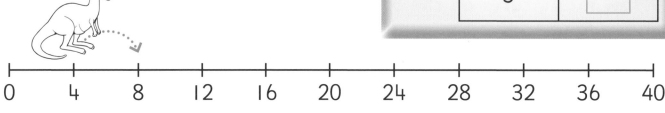

| 0 | 4 | 8 | 12 | 16 | 20 | 24 | 28 | 32 | 36 | 40 |

2. a) Roo starts at number 4. He takes 1 jump. Where does he land? **8**

b) Roo starts at number 12. He takes 2 jumps. Where does he land? ☐

c) Roo starts at number 8. He takes 4 jumps. Where does he land? ☐

d) Roo starts at number 16. He takes 2 jumps. Where does he land? ☐

e) Roo starts at number 20. He takes 3 jumps. Where does he land? ☐

f) Roo starts at number 28. He takes 2 jumps. Where does he land? ☐

g) Roo starts at number 32. He takes 1 jump. Where does he land? ☐

Algebra – Extending and Using Patterns

Counting in Fives

1. **Draw five petals on each flower.**

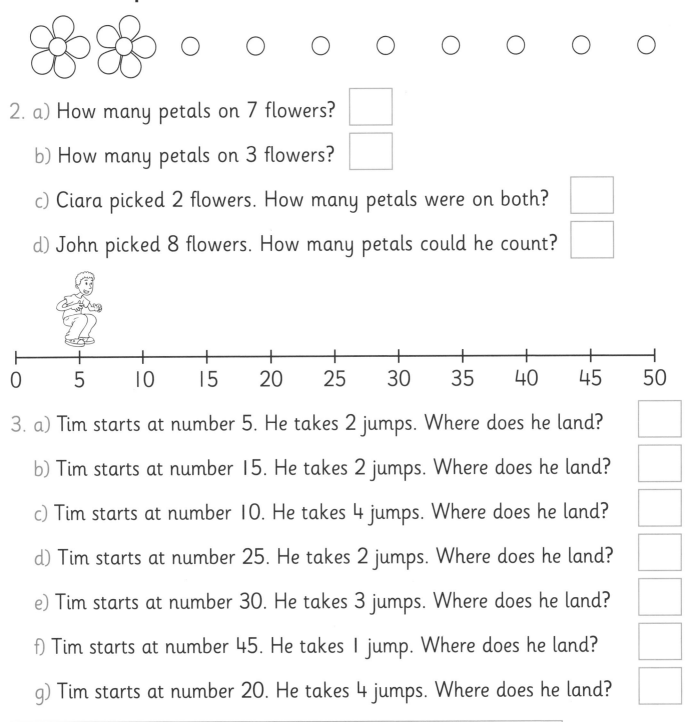

2. a) How many petals on 7 flowers? ☐

   b) How many petals on 3 flowers? ☐

   c) Ciara picked 2 flowers. How many petals were on both? ☐

   d) John picked 8 flowers. How many petals could he count? ☐

3. a) Tim starts at number 5. He takes 2 jumps. Where does he land? ☐

   b) Tim starts at number 15. He takes 2 jumps. Where does he land? ☐

   c) Tim starts at number 10. He takes 4 jumps. Where does he land? ☐

   d) Tim starts at number 25. He takes 2 jumps. Where does he land? ☐

   e) Tim starts at number 30. He takes 3 jumps. Where does he land? ☐

   f) Tim starts at number 45. He takes 1 jump. Where does he land? ☐

   g) Tim starts at number 20. He takes 4 jumps. Where does he land? ☐

4. **In your copy**

   a) Write all the numbers from 2 to 20 counting in twos.

   b) Write all the numbers from 4 to 40 counting in fours.

   c) Write all the numbers from 5 to 50 counting in fives.

Finished Early? Now try counting backwards!

Counting in Threes

1. **Draw three black spots on each bug.**

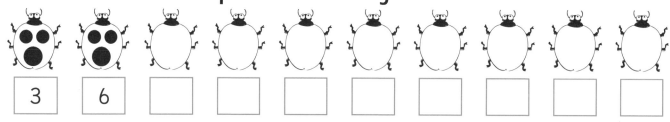

3	6								

2. a) How many spots on 2 bugs? ☐

   b) 4 bugs have ☐ spots.

   c) How many spots on 6 bugs? ☐

   d) 3 bugs have ☐ spots.

   e) How many spots on 10 bugs? ☐

   f) 7 bugs have ☐ spots.

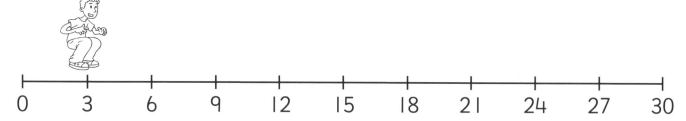

3. a) Tim starts at 3. He makes 2 jumps. He lands on ☐.

   b) Tim starts on 9. He makes 3 jumps. He lands on ☐.

   c) Tim starts on 6. He makes 1 jump. He lands on ☐.

   d) Tim starts on 15. He makes 4 jumps. He lands on ☐.

   e) Tim starts on 21. He makes 3 jumps. He lands on ☐.

   f) Tim starts on 12. He makes 5 jumps. He lands on ☐.

   g) Tim starts on 24. He makes 2 jumps. He lands on ☐.

4. **Add 3 to these numbers.**

   6 ☐   12 ☐   9 ☐   18 ☐   21 ☐

   3 ☐   34 ☐   0 ☐   15 ☐   27 ☐

Counting in Sixes

1. **Draw 6 leaves on each tree.**

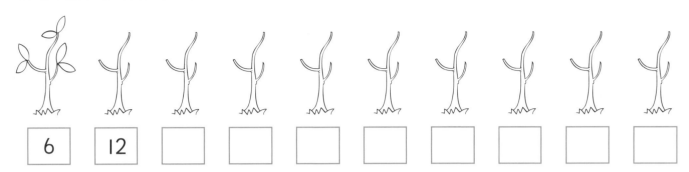

6	12								

2. **One tree has 6 leaves. How many leaves on:**

a) 2 trees? ☐   b) 5 trees? ☐   c) 3 trees? ☐

d) 6 trees? ☐   e) 4 trees? ☐   f) 10 trees? ☐

g) 9 trees? ☐   h) 7 trees? ☐   i) 8 trees? ☐

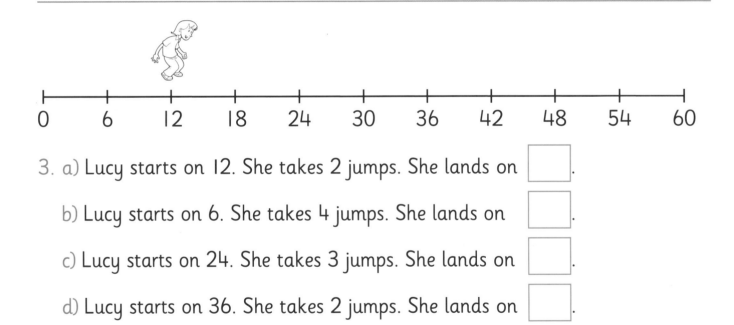

0   6   12   18   24   30   36   42   48   54   60

3. a) Lucy starts on 12. She takes 2 jumps. She lands on ☐.

b) Lucy starts on 6. She takes 4 jumps. She lands on ☐.

c) Lucy starts on 24. She takes 3 jumps. She lands on ☐.

d) Lucy starts on 36. She takes 2 jumps. She lands on ☐.

e) Lucy starts on 42. She takes 1 jump. She lands on ☐.

4. **Write the missing numerals.**

a) 6, 12, ☐, 24, 30, 36

b) 18, 24, 30, 36, ☐, 48

More Counting

1. Draw 4 legs on each chair.

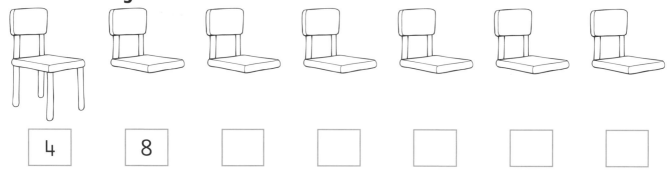

| 4 | 8 | | | | | |

---

2. One chair has 4 legs. How many legs on:

a) 3 chairs? ☐   b) 2 chairs? ☐   c) 5 chairs? ☐

d) 6 chairs? ☐   e) 4 chairs? ☐   f) 7 chairs? ☐

3.

a) 16 wings = ☐ bees   b) 20 wings = ☐ bees

4.

a) 18 spots = ☐ giraffes   b) 30 spots = ☐ giraffes

5.

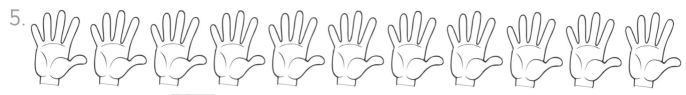

a) 15 fingers = ☐ hands   b) 35 fingers = ☐ hands

Recap

• I can recognise patterns.

• I can count in twos, threes, fours, fives and sixes.

1. How much in each purse?

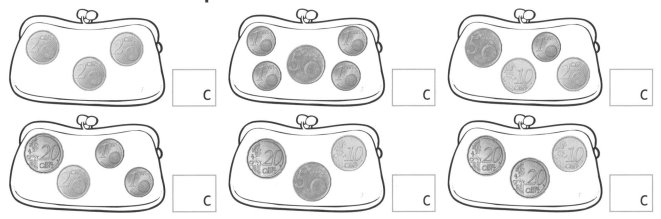

☐ c   ☐ c   ☐ c

☐ c   ☐ c   ☐ c

2. Draw coins in each purse to make the correct amount.

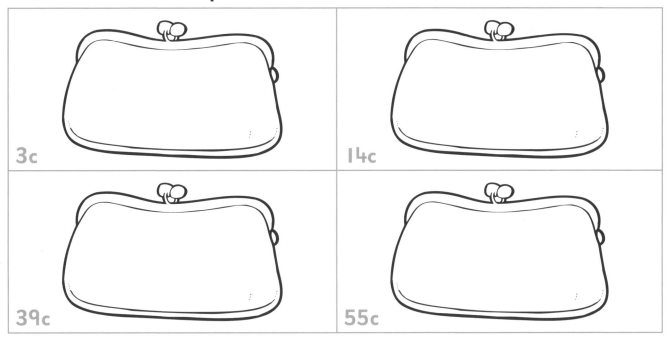

3c

14c

39c

55c

3. What 2 coins would you use?

3c	◯ ◯	22c	◯ ◯
7c	◯ ◯	25c	◯ ◯
11c	◯ ◯	30c	◯ ◯
15c	◯ ◯	40c	◯ ◯

4. Find the change from 50c.

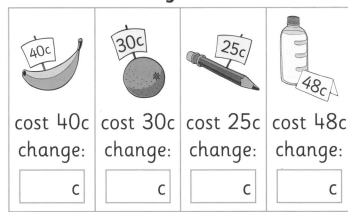

40c	30c	25c	48c
cost 40c	cost 30c	cost 25c	cost 48c
change:	change:	change:	change:
☐ c	☐ c	☐ c	☐ c

Strand: Measures
Curriculum Objectives:
Recognise, exchange and use coins up to the value of €2.00;
write the value of a group of coins up to the value of €2.00;
record money as cents and euros.

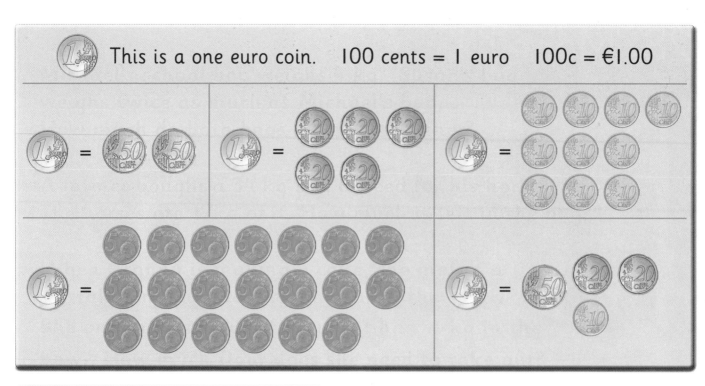

This is a one euro coin.   100 cents = 1 euro   100c = €1.00

💡 Use your coins to help you.

1. **Write the amount on the coins and colour.**

€1 = 50 + 20 + 10 + 10 + ○

€1 = 50 + 20 + 10 + 10 + 5 + ○

€1 = 20 + 20 + 20 + 10 + ○ + ○

€1 = 10 + 10 + 10 + 10 + 10 + 10 + 10 + 10 + 10 + ○

€1 = ○ + 20 + 20 + 10

€1 = 50 + ○ + ○ + 5 + 5

2. **Sally had 50c. She got another fifty cent coin from her Dad.**
   How much money has Sally? ☐ c

3. **Jack has 2 twenty cent coins. Amy has 3 ten cent coins.**
   How much money have they altogether? ☐ c

Finished Early?
In your copy draw six different ways to make €1.

Change from €1.00

The biscuits cost 94c and you have €1. How much change will you get?
Count on to the nearest 5c or 10c.

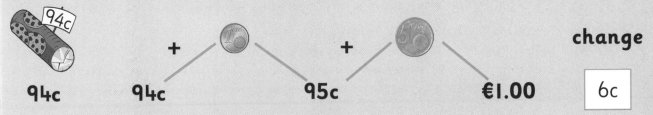

94c + (1c) + (5c) → change

94c   94c   95c   €1.00   **6c**

The change is 1c and 5c. This makes 6c altogether.

1. **Find the change from one euro (€1.00).**   change

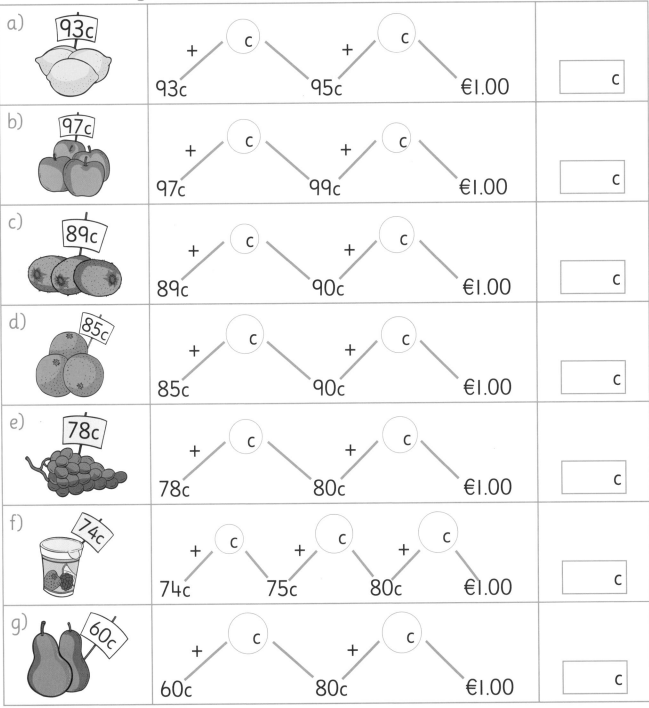

a) 93c   + (c) + (c)   93c   95c   €1.00   ☐ c

b) 97c   + (c) + (c)   97c   99c   €1.00   ☐ c

c) 89c   + (c) + (c)   89c   90c   €1.00   ☐ c

d) 85c   + (c) + (c)   85c   90c   €1.00   ☐ c

e) 78c   + (c) + (c)   78c   80c   €1.00   ☐ c

f) 74c   + (c) + (c) + (c)   74c   75c   80c   €1.00   ☐ c

g) 60c   + (c) + (c)   60c   80c   €1.00   ☐ c

Writing Amounts of Money

Can you write amounts of money using a € sign?

100c = €1.00 | 150c = €1.50 | 125c = €1.25

Remember to use only one symbol

143c ✓   €1.43 ✓

€1.43c ✗

1. **How much money is in each purse? Write the answer using the € symbol.**

€ __1__ . __00__   € _____ . _____   € _____ . _____   € _____ . _____

€ _____ . _____   € _____ . _____   € _____ . _____   € _____ . _____

2. **Write the price tags using the € symbol.**   117c = €1.17

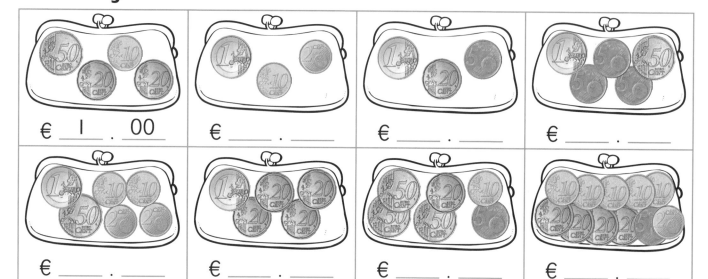

183c = €1.83   152c =   187c =   135c =

141c =   166c =   199c =   174c =

118c =   140c =   104c =   109c =

3. a) What is the cost of the bread and jam? [ ]   €1   67c

   b) Dan bought three tickets for the cinema. Each ticket cost 50c. How much did he spend? [ ]

   c) Add one euro coin, one fifty cent coin and a two cent coin. What is the total? [ ]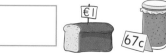

More About Change

When calculating change, count on to the nearest 5c or 10c and then jump in tens.

cost	change in coins from 20c	total change
16c		4c

The orange costs 16c. You need to add on 2c and 2c to get to 20c.
The coins you add on are the change. 2c + 2c = 4c. So the change is 4c.

1. **Find the change from 20c.**

cost	change in coins	total change
19c	(1c)	1c
17c	( ) ( )	
15c	( )	

2. **Find the change from 50c.**

cost	change in coins	total change
40c	( )	
35c	( ) ( )	
28c	( ) ( )	

3. **Find the change from €1.00.**

cost	change in coins	total change
89c	( ) ( )	
92c	( ) ( ) ( )	
78c	( ) ( )	

Money

Wandy Witch's Candy Corner	
Wanda Bar	20c
Wicked Gobstoppers	15c
Fizzy Eyeballs	25c
Black Cat Gumdrops	10c
Spooky Toffee	40c

1. **Work out how much change you will get from €1.**

💡 Use your coins and don't forget to count on.

items	cost	change from €1
1 Wanda Bar	20c	80c
2 Spooky Toffees		
2 Fizzy Eyeballs		
3 Wicked Gobstoppers		
4 Black Cat Gumdrops and 1 Wanda Bar		
1 Spooky Toffee and 1 Wicked Gobstopper		
7 Black Cat Gumdrops and 1 Fizzy Eyeball		

Puzzler

Mandy has seven coins in her pocket. She has four gold coins and three bronze coins. How much money do you think Mandy has? Find all the possible totals.
What is the largest and smallest amount Mandy could have?

Recap

- I can write money as euros or cents.
- I can add groups of coins.
- I can work out change from 20c, 50c and €1.

29. 3-D Shapes

| cuboid | cube | cylinder | sphere | cone |

1. What 3-D shapes can you see in these real-life pictures?

_____   _____   _____   _____   _____

_____   _____   _____   _____   _____

2. Write the name of the shape.

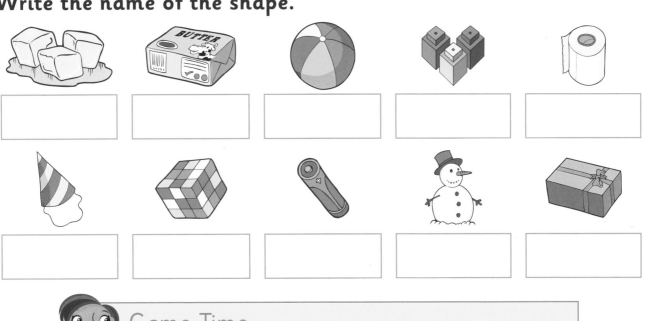

Game Time

Play 'I Spy Shapes' in the classroom: 'I spy with my little eye something in the shape of a . . .'.

Strand: Shape and Space
Curriculum Objectives:
Describe, compare and name 3-D shapes – cube, cuboid, sphere, cylinder and cone;

discuss the use of 3-D shapes in the environment;
explore the relationship between 2-D and 3-D shapes.

1. **Trace and name the 3-D shapes.**

| cube |
| cuboid |
| sphere |
| cylinder |
| cone |

_____ _____ _____ _____ _____

2. **Use your 3-D shapes to investigate.**

3-D shapes	Does it roll? ✓ or ✗	Does it slide? ✓ or ✗	Can it stack? ✓ or ✗

3. The _____ , _____ and _____ can **roll**.

The _____, _____, _____ and

_____ can **slide**.

The _____, _____ and _____ can **stack**.

The _____ can roll, slide **and** stack.

Puzzler

How many square faces in this design? ▢

How many corners altogether? ▢

How many edges can you count? ▢

Remember to count the hidden faces, corners and edges.

3-D Shapes

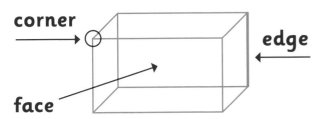

corner

edge

face

A 3-D shape is not flat. It has **faces**, **corners** and **edges**.

Its faces are 2-D shapes.

1. **Use your 3-D shapes to investigate.**

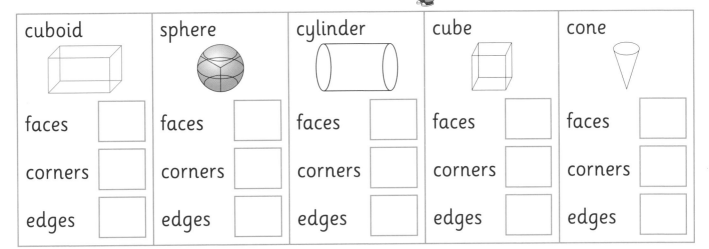

cuboid	sphere	cylinder	cube	cone
faces	faces	faces	faces	faces
corners	corners	corners	corners	corners
edges	edges	edges	edges	edges

2. **Trace around the 3-D shapes. Draw around...**

the base of a cone and you get a	one of the the faces of a cube and you get a
the base of a cylinder and you get a	one of the long faces of a cuboid and you get a

Recap

- I can recognise and name 3-D shapes.
- I know the number of faces, edges and corners in each 3-D shape.
- I know which shapes can slide, roll and stack.

30. Addition 4

Big Doubles

$11 + 11 =$

$10 + 10 + 1 + 1 =$

$20 + 2 = 22$

 Add the bundles of ten first, then add the units.

$12 + 12 =$

$10 + 10 + 2 + 2 =$

$20 + 4 = 24$

Now you try.

1.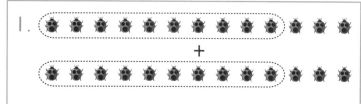

$13 + 13$

$10 + \boxed{} + 3 + \boxed{}$

$\boxed{} + \boxed{} = \boxed{}$

2.

$14 + 14$

$\boxed{} + \boxed{} + \boxed{} + 4$

$\boxed{} + \boxed{} = \boxed{}$

3. $12 + 12$

$\boxed{} + \boxed{} + \boxed{} + \boxed{}$

$\boxed{} + \boxed{} = \boxed{}$

4. $15 + 15$

$\boxed{} + \boxed{} + \boxed{} + \boxed{}$

$\boxed{} + \boxed{} = \boxed{}$

Strand: Number
Curriculum Objectives:
Develop mental strategies for addition facts;
add numbers with and without renaming to 99;
construct number sentences.

Adding Using Groups of Tens

Examples

 Split the numbers into tens and units.
Put the tens together. Put the units together.

24 + 32

24 = 20 and 4   32 = 30 and 2

= 20 + 30 + 4 + 2

= 50 + 6 = 56

Now try these:

1. 74 + 25

     70 + 20 + 4 + 5

     ☐ + ☐ = ☐

2. 28 + 61

     20 + 60 + 8 + 1

     ☐ + ☐ = ☐

3. 81 + 15

     ☐ + ☐ + ☐ + ☐

     ☐ + ☐ = ☐

4. 34 + 23

     ☐ + ☐ + ☐ + ☐

     ☐ + ☐ = ☐

5. 22 + 27

     ☐ + ☐ + ☐ + ☐

     ☐ + ☐ = ☐

6. 44 + 52

     ☐ + ☐ + ☐ + ☐

     ☐ + ☐ = ☐

7. 73 + 16

     ☐ + ☐ + ☐ + ☐

     ☐ + ☐ = ☐

8. 62 + 37

     ☐ + ☐ + ☐ + ☐

     ☐ + ☐ = ☐

9. 24 + 65

     ☐ + ☐ + ☐ + ☐

     ☐ + ☐ = ☐

10. 51 + 48

     ☐ + ☐ + ☐ + ☐

     ☐ + ☐ = ☐

Let's try 29 + 5.
Think of the nearest 10.
29 wants to be 30, so it takes 1 from 5.
29 has changed to 30 and 5 has changed to 4.
29 + 5 = 30 + 4

29 + 5

30 + 4 = 34

1. **Try these addition sums.**

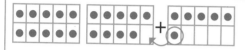

19 + 6 =

20 + 5 = ☐

29 + 7 =

30 + 6 = ☐

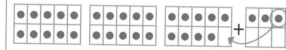

29 + 3 =

30 + ___ = ☐

29 + 8 =

___ + ___ = ☐

2. **Now try these.**

9 + 5 = ☐	9 + 7 = ☐	9 + 4 = ☐	9 + 9 = ☐
19 + 5 = ☐	19 + 7 = ☐	19 + 4 = ☐	19 + 9 = ☐
29 + 5 = ☐	29 + 7 = ☐	29 + 4 = ☐	29 + 9 = ☐
39 + 5 = ☐	39 + 7 = ☐	39 + 4 = ☐	39 + 9 = ☐
9 + 2 = ☐	9 + 3 = ☐	9 + 6 = ☐	9 + 8 = ☐
19 + 2 = ☐	19 + 3 = ☐	19 + 6 = ☐	19 + 8 = ☐
29 + 2 = ☐	29 + 3 = ☐	29 + 6 = ☐	29 + 8 = ☐
39 + 2 = ☐	39 + 3 = ☐	39 + 6 = ☐	39 + 8 = ☐

Can you see a pattern? _____

1. Add to solve the riddle.

What dinosaur could jump higher than a house?

Number line: 0 1 2 3 4 5 6 7 8 9 10 11 12 13 14 15 16 17 18 19 20

41	75	63
+38	+16	+28
79		
A		

35	26
+58	+41

47	38	26	35
+37	+39	+54	+54

42	46	28	17	33	52
+35	+47	+48	+68	+47	+33

68	28	27	26
+ 4	+51	+69	+58

19	9	13	29
+39	+67	+76	+35

F	E	M	A	S	C	O	H	J	L	U	N	P	T
67	80	89	79	85	72	93	77	58	91	76	96	64	84

Puzzler

There are 12 numbers in the box between 27 and 72. The numbers increase by 3 each time. Can you work out the numbers that are missing?

36	30	48	42
27	39	54	69
57	66	72	63

Hint: Begin with the lowest number.

[ ] [ ] [ ] [ ]

Word Problems

At the Airport

1. **43 people flew to London on Monday morning.**

   37 people flew there on Monday afternoon.

   How many people went to London on Monday? ☐

   Work it out here

t	u

2. **73 pilots wore a blue uniform.**

   19 pilots wore a green uniform.

   ☐ pilots wore a uniform.

t	u

3. **28 aeroplanes flew into Dublin airport during the day.**

   37 flew in that night.

   ☐ aeroplanes flew into Dublin altogether.

t	u

4. **56 people bought tickets for their trip online.**

   26 people bought tickets at the desk.

   ☐ tickets were sold altogether.

t	u

5. **38 men and 36 women travelled to Poland.**

   How many went to Poland? ☐

t	u

6. **25 books were sold at the airport shop.**

   68 newspapers were sold also.

   ☐ books and newspapers were sold altogether.

t	u

At the Bakery

1. **The baker baked 28 scones in the morning.**
   In the afternoon he baked 12 scones.

   How many did he bake?

   ☐ + ☐ = ☐

   Work it out here

	t	u
+		

2. **Jessica sold 19 toffee apples on Friday.**
   She sold 11 more on Saturday.

   How many toffee apples did she sell?

   ☐ + ☐ = ☐

   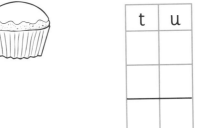

	t	u

3. **Mammy bought 18 flapjacks for Evan's party.**
   She bought 25 pieces of biscuit cake.

   Add up everything Mammy bought for the party.

   ☐ + ☐ = ☐

	t	u

4. **35 buns were covered in chocolate.**
   15 buns had icing on them.

   How many buns were for sale altogether?

   ☐ + ☐ = ☐

   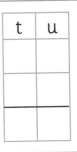

	t	u

5. **There were 27 cherries in the big cherry cake.**
   In the small cherry cake there were 19 cherries.

   How many cherries were there in the two cherry cakes?

   ☐ + ☐ = ☐

	t	u

Recap

- I can work out addition sums in my head. ◯ ◯ ◯
- I can do word problems. ◯ ◯ ◯

31. Subtraction 4

Key Words

subtract −	add +
how many more? how many fewer? what is the difference?	altogether in total

1. **Mary bought 20 sweets. Jane bought 12 sweets.**

   How many more **sweets than Jane did Mary buy?**

t	u

2. **John had 17 marbles. Mark had 15 marbles.**

   How many marbles did they have altogether?

t	u

3. **Nessa needs 35 party hats for all the children coming to her party. She has 18 hats.**

   How many more **does Nessa need?**

t	u

4. **There are 53 girls in Sunny Days Summer Camp. There are 72 boys.**

   What is the difference **between the number of boys and girls at the camp?**

t	u

5. **In Tom's class 8 children have a pet dog and 23 have a pet cat.**

   How many children altogether **have pets?**

t	u

Strand: Number
Curriculum Objectives:
Develop an understanding of subtraction as deducting, as complementing and as difference;
develop and recall mental strategies for subtraction 0–20;
construct number sentences involving subtraction of whole numbers; solve problems involving subtraction;
subtract numbers without and with renaming within 99;
use the symbols +, −, =, <, >;
solve one-step problems involving subtraction.

Word Problems

1. In a car shop, there are 45 silver cars and 29 red cars.

   What is the difference between the number of silver cars and the number of red cars?

t	u

2. Annie bought a packet of 52 playing cards. She gave her brother Joe 27 of them.

   How many cards has Annie now?

t	u

3. Jill ran for 35 minutes and then she walked for 19 minutes.
   What is the difference between the time she spent running and the time she spent walking?

t	u

4. Jack has 17 football cards of his favourite players. His best friend Robert has 19 more than Jack.

   How many football cards does Robert have?

t	u

5. When Michael was seven, 12 children came to his party. On his next party, when he was eight, 15 more children came than when he was seven.

   How many fewer children came to his seventh party?

t	u

Subtraction

0 1 2 3 4 5 6 7 8 9 10 11 12 13 14 15 16 17 18 19 20

1.
19 − 6 = ☐   15 − 9 = ☐   18 − 4 = ☐

20 − 10 = ☐   11 − 8 = ☐   12 − 5 = ☐

15 − 6 = ☐   17 − 9 = ☐   19 − 8 = ☐

18 − 5 = ☐   11 − 7 = ☐   20 − 9 = ☐

2.
13 − ☐ = 7   16 − ☐ = 12   14 − ☐ = 5

19 − ☐ = 10   15 − ☐ = 11   13 − ☐ = 6

20 − ☐ = 11   13 − ☐ = 4   14 − ☐ = 7

15 − ☐ = 5   12 − ☐ = 7   17 − ☐ = 9

3.

t u	t u	t u	t u	t u	t u
3 4	2 3	3 8	4 9	5 4	4 4
− 1 2	− 1 1	− 1 6	− 1 4	− 1 0	− 1 2
☐	☐	☐	☐	☐	☐

4.

t u	t u	t u	t u	t u	t u
4 8	3 7	2 4	6 8	4 9	5 5
− 1 4	− 1 5	− 8	− 2 8	− 1 7	− 2 2
☐	☐	☐	☐	☐	☐

5.

t u	t u	t u	t u	t u	t u
3 5	4 2	3 8	4 5	3 8	6 4
− 1 8	− 1 4	− 1 9	− 2 6	− 2 9	− 2 6
☐	☐	☐	☐	☐	☐

6.

t u	t u	t u	t u	t u	t u
6 8	4 1	6 0	5 3	4 0	5 7
− 2 9	− 1 5	− 2 5	− 2 5	− 2 9	− 4 8
☐	☐	☐	☐	☐	☐

Subtraction

1.

☐ – 4 = 15	☐ – 3 = 10	☐ – 8 = 8	☐ – 7 = 9
☐ – 5 = 8	☐ – 4 = 12	☐ – 6 = 10	☐ – 10 = 10
☐ – 9 = 3	☐ – 6 = 8	☐ – 5 = 5	☐ – 8 = 4
☐ – 10 = 8	☐ – 9 = 11	☐ – 4 = 13	☐ – 9 = 9

Crack the Codes!

2. Where do cows go on their holidays?

y	r	o	m	k
67	75	82	89	71
– 52	– 58	– 6	– 69	– 55
___	___	___	___	___

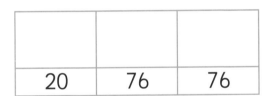

20	76	76

15	76	17	16

3. What has teeth but cannot eat?

o	b	a	c	m
63	81	40	71	57
– 49	– 25	– 9	– 55	– 4
___	___	___	___	___

31

16	14	53	56

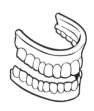

Crack the Code

1. **Why does a giraffe have a long neck?**

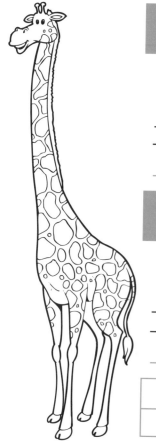

m	b	a	s	h	c
t u	t u	t u	t u	t u	t u
8 3	6 0	8 3	8 8	3 2	7 2
− 6 4	− 6	− 1 6	− 5 0	− 2 5	− 5 6

e	f	u	l	i	t
t u	t u	t u	t u	t u	t u
8 7	7 4	7 9	8 5	7 8	2 3
− 4 3	− 5 7	− 5 4	− 7 2	− 5 2	− 1 5

54	44	16	67	25	38	44

7	26	38

17	44	44	8

38	19	44	13	13

Puzzler

The teacher had 50 stickers.

The first child took one sticker, the second child took 2 stickers, the third took 3 and so on. How many children got stickers?

Recap

- I know which words in problems tell me to subtract.
- I can subtract with and without renaming.

○ ○ ○
○ ○ ○

32. Place Value 2

Write the Number

hundreds	tens	units	number?
			134

Strand: Number
Curriculum Objective:
Explore, identify and record place value 0–199.

1. **Show these numbers on your abacus.**

a)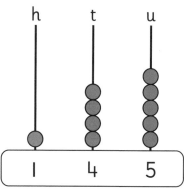

h	t	u
1	4	5

b)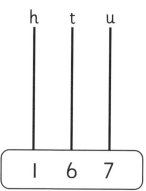

h	t	u
1	6	7

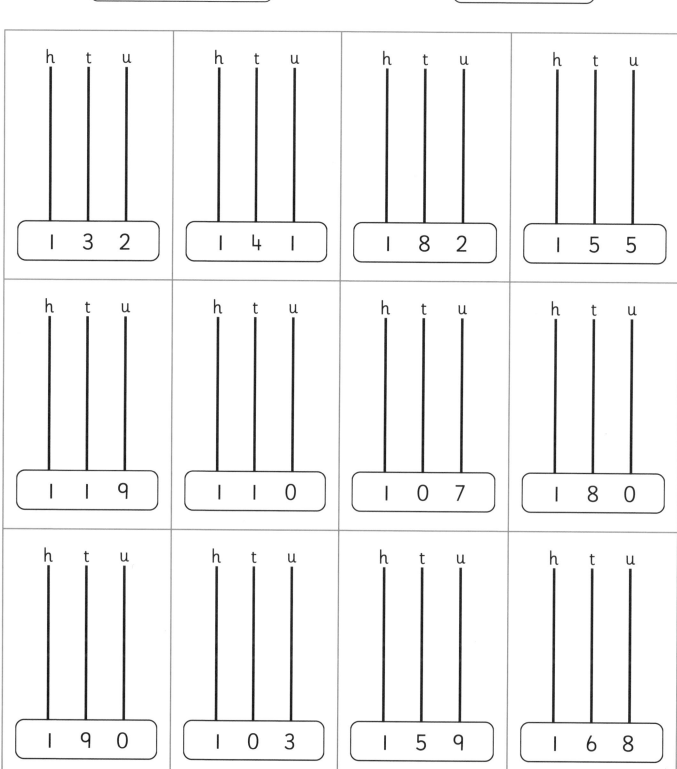

h	t	u
1	3	2

h	t	u
1	4	1

h	t	u
1	8	2

h	t	u
1	5	5

h	t	u
1	1	9

h	t	u
1	1	0

h	t	u
1	0	7

h	t	u
1	8	0

h	t	u
1	9	0

h	t	u
1	0	3

h	t	u
1	5	9

h	t	u
1	6	8

Place Value

1. **Write the number shown on the abacus.**

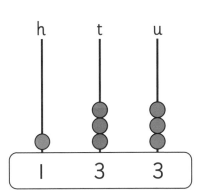

1	3	3

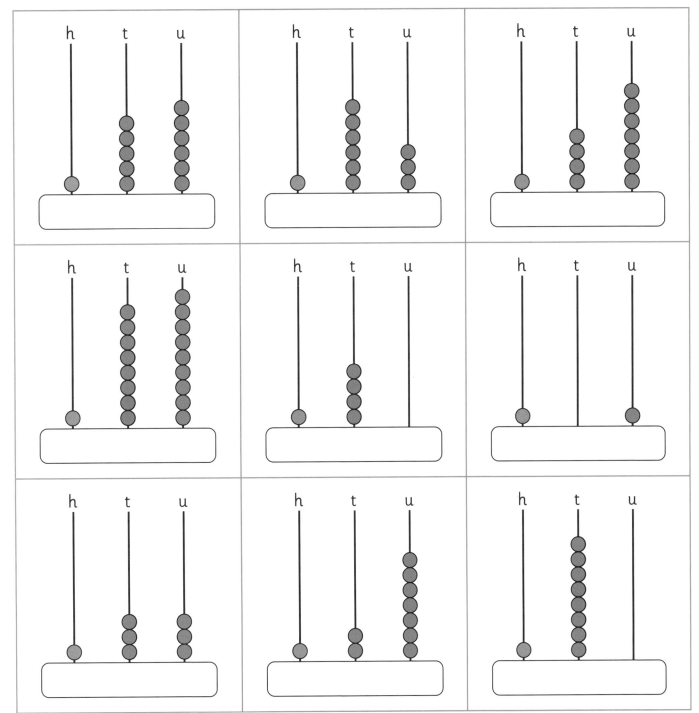

2. I hundred 6 tens and 5 units = ☐

   I hundred 8 tens and 2 units = ☐

Let's Rename

 Remember: one ten is equal to ten units.

tens	units		tens	units
⊞⊞	▫ ▫ ▫ ▫ ▫	→	⊞	▫ ▫ ▫ ▫ ▫ ▫ ▫ ▫ ▫ ▫ ▫ ▫ ▫ ▫ ▫
2 tens	5 units	→	1 ten	15 units

When you rename a number, you take away one ten and you put it with the units.

1. **Now try these.**

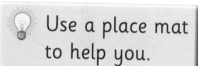
Use a place mat to help you.

39	renames to	2	tens and	19	units
47	renames to		tens and		units
26	renames to		ten and		units
85	renames to		tens and		units
49	renames to		tens and		units
23	renames to		ten and		units
35	renames to		tens and		units
17	renames to		tens and		units
40	renames to		tens and		units
56	renames to		tens and		units
79	renames to		tens and		units
81	renames to		tens and		units
24	renames to		ten and		units
58	renames to		tens and		units

Crack the Code!

1. a = the tens number in 131   a = ☐

   o = the units number in 127   o = ☐

   t = the hundreds number in 158   t = ☐

   c = the tens number in 87   c = ☐

   r = the tens number in 56   r = ☐

Use your answers to solve the code . . .

1	5	3	8	1	7	5

2. **Now draw a picture of the word in the box below.**

Puzzler
Fill in the missing numbers

	☐	4	5
+	2	☐	7
	3	9	☐

Recap
- I know all about hundreds, tens and units.
- I can show hundreds, tens and units on a place mat.
- I can rename.

101–200

This is a 100-square numbered from 101 to 200.

1. Fill in the missing numbers.

101	102		104	105	106		108	109	110
111	112	113	114		116	117	118	119	120
	122	123	124	125	126	127	128		130
131	132	133		135	136	137	138	139	140
141	142	143	144	145	146	147		149	150
151	152	153	154	155		157	158	159	160
161	162	163	164	165	166	167	168	169	
171	172	173	174	175	176		178	179	180
181		183	184	185		187	188	189	190
191	192		194	195	196	197	198		200

2. Colour these numbers yellow.

- one hundred and fourteen
- one hundred and thirty-one
- one hundred and twenty-five
- one hundred and forty-six
- one hundred and fifty-nine
- one hundred and eighty-three
- one hundred and sixty-two
- one hundred and seventy-eight
- one hundred and ninety-four

3. Write the house number that comes after these numbers.

| 111 | | 149 | | 166 | | 104 | | 135 | |

4. Write the door numbers that come before these numbers.

| | 117 | | 108 | | 156 | | 140 | | 192 | | 169 |

Recap

- I can read and write numbers to 200.
- I can order numbers to 200.

Strand: Number
Curriculum Objectives:
Count the number of objects in a set.
Read, write and order numerals 0–199.

34. Area

The green plate has a greater **area** than the yellow plate.

The **area** of a shape is the amount of surface that the shape covers.

1. a) Colour the square with the greatest surface area red.
   b) Colour the square with the smallest surface area blue.
   c) Colour the squares with the same surface area green.

2. a) Colour the triangle with the greatest surface area red.
   b) Colour the triangle with the smallest surface area blue.
   c) Colour the triangles with the same surface area green.

3. | a) Name or draw 2 things that have a greater area than your copy. | b) Name or draw 2 things that have a smaller area than your classroom door. |
   |---|---|
   | | |

Puzzler

Look at this shape. How many different squares with an area of four squares can you find?

Strand: Measures
Curriculum Objective:
Estimate and measure area using non-standard units.

Area

1. **Use different objects to cover the top of your table.**
   Estimate **first and then** measure **the** area.

object		estimate	measurement
maths books			
copies			
lunch boxes			
pencil cases			
playing cards			

2. **True or false?** ✓ **or** ✗

   a) It took more playing cards than maths books to cover the table.

   b) I needed more copies than playing cards to cover the table.

   c) The area of a shape is the amount of space inside the lines.

At Home

3. **How many do I need to cover my bed?**

object	estimate	measurement
pillows		
cushions		

Finished Early?
Draw a house in your squared maths copy. What is the area of your house? ☐ squares

---

Recap

• I know that the **area** of a shape is the space inside it. ◯ ◯ ◯

• I can measure surface area with many different things. ◯ ◯ ◯

• I know that some things are better at covering surfaces
  than others. ◯ ◯ ◯

35. Check-up 4

1. **How many legs do 6 dogs have?** [ ]

2. **Write the following using the € sign.**

   123c = € [ ]   104c = € [ ]   189c = € [ ]   115c = € [ ]

3. **Fill in the missing numbers.**

[ ]		
26		
36		

   | [ ] |
   | 54 |
   | [ ] |

	[ ]	
78	
87	

[ ]	
	90
	[ ]

4. **What change will you have from €1? Write the correct amount.**

cost	change in coins	total change
79c ○ ○		
44c ○ ○ ○		

5. 10 + 10 = [ ]   13 + 13 = [ ]   12 + 12 = [ ]   14 + 14 = [ ]

6.
t u	t u	t u	t u
5 3	7 7	4 4	7 3
+ 3 8	+ 2 8	+ 1 7	+ 1 3
_____	_____	_____	_____

7.
t u	t u	t u	t u
2 1	5 6	3 7	4 6
− 1 9	− 3 6	− 2 8	− 3 8
_____	_____	_____	_____

8. **Name these shapes:**

   _____ _____ _____ _____

9. **Jake the farmer had 63 sheep. He sold 29.**

   How many sheep has Jake now? [ ]

Curriculum Objective:
To revise concepts that were explored in units 27–34.

36. Subtraction with the 101–200 Square

1. Fill in the missing numbers.

101		103				107			
			114				118		
		123			126			129	
			135						140
	142		144						
151						157			
		163					168		
				176			179		
	182				187				190
191								199	

2. Look at the 101–200 square. Fill in the missing numerals.

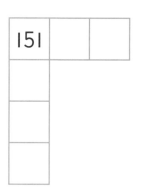

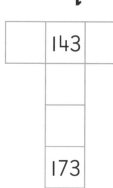

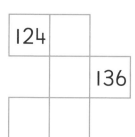

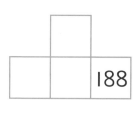

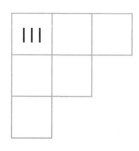

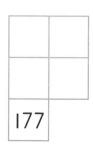

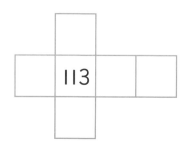

Strand: Number
Curriculum Objectives:
Construct number sentences involving subtraction of whole numbers;
solve problems involving subtraction;
subtract numbers without and with renaming within 199;
solve one-step problems involving subtraction.

Subtraction

101	102	103	104	105	106	107	108	109	110
111	112	113	114	115	116	117	118	119	120
121	122	123	124	125	126	127	128	129	130
131	132	133	134	135	136	137	138	139	140
141	142	143	144	145	146	147	148	149	150
151	152	153	154	155	156	157	158	159	160
161	162	163	164	165	166	167	168	169	170
171	172	173	174	175	176	177	178	179	180
181	182	183	184	185	186	187	188	189	190
191	192	193	194	195	196	197	198	199	200

124 − 3 = 121
Start on 124.
Jump back 3 spaces.
You land on **121**.

1. **Use your 101–200 square to help you subtract.**

a) 145 − 8 = ☐   176 − 9 = ☐   115 − 10 = ☐

b) 137 − 7 = ☐   183 − 15 = ☐   194 − 12 = ☐

c) 162 − 5 = ☐   123 − 6 = ☐   138 − 4 = ☐

d) 161 − 11 = ☐   174 − 13 = ☐   153 − 9 = ☐

e) 131 − 9 = ☐   185 − 7 = ☐   196 − 10 = ☐

f) 147 − 9 = ☐   182 − 9 = ☐   171 − 9 = ☐

g) 154 − 7 = ☐   179 − 8 = ☐   147 − 8 = ☐

2. a) Start on 119 and jump back 9 spaces. You land on ☐

b) Start on 126 and jump back 8 spaces. You land on ☐

c) Start on 157 and jump back 6 spaces. You land on ☐

d) Start on 126 and jump back 7 spaces. You land on ☐

e) Start on 120 and jump back 8 spaces. You land on ☐

Subtraction

101	102	103	104	105	106	107	108	109	110
111	112	113	114	115	116	117	118	119	120
121	122	123	124	125	126	127	128	129	130
131	132	133	134	135	136	137	138	139	140
141	142	143	144	145	146	147	148	149	150
151	152	153	154	155	156	157	158	159	160
161	162	163	164	165	166	167	168	169	170
171	172	173	174	175	176	177	178	179	180
181	182	183	184	185	186	187	188	189	190
191	192	193	194	195	196	197	198	199	200

1. **In pairs, find the following numerals on your 101-200 square:**

   135, 142, 193, 160, 174, 188

2. **Use your 101–200 square to answer the following:**

   a) $198 - 8 =$ ☐ $190 - 7 =$ ☐ $193 - 6 =$ ☐ $187 - 5 =$ ☐

   b) $188 - 8 =$ ☐ $180 - 7 =$ ☐ $183 - 6 =$ ☐ $177 - 5 =$ ☐

   c) $178 - 8 =$ ☐ $170 - 7 =$ ☐ $173 - 6 =$ ☐ $167 - 5 =$ ☐

   d) $168 - 8 =$ ☐ $160 - 7 =$ ☐ $163 - 6 =$ ☐ $157 - 5 =$ ☐

   e) $158 - 8 =$ ☐ $150 - 7 =$ ☐ $153 - 6 =$ ☐ $147 - 5 =$ ☐

   f) $148 - 8 =$ ☐ $140 - 7 =$ ☐ $143 - 6 =$ ☐ $137 - 5 =$ ☐

Puzzler

Which digit appears the most on the 101–200 square?

Recap

- I can use the 101–200 square to help me subtract. ○ ○ ○
- I can recognise number patterns on the 101–200 square. ○ ○ ○

37. Capacity

1. **Colour the container that holds the most water** yellow.
2. **Colour the container that holds the least water** blue.
3. **Circle one container that holds more water than the cup.**
4. **Cross out a container that holds less water than the bottle.**
5. **Estimate, then measure how many cups it takes to fill each container.**

container	estimate	answer

6. **Draw the containers in order of their capacity below.**

➡ In order of capacity ➡

Strand: Measures
Curriculum Objectives:
Estimate, compare, measure and record the capacity of a wide variety of containers using non-standard units;

select and use appropriate non-standard measuring units and instruments;
estimate, measure and record capacity using litres, half-litres and quarter-litres and solve simple problems.

How Much Is a Litre?

1 litre mark

1. **Find containers that hold less than 1 litre and more than 1 litre.**

less than 1 litre	1 litre	more than 1 litre
	MILK	

2. **Estimate and measure the capacity of each container.**

container	estimates			The correct answer was . . .
	less than 1 litre	about 1 litre	more than 1 litre	
	✓			less than 1 litre

Capacity – $\frac{1}{2}$ Litre

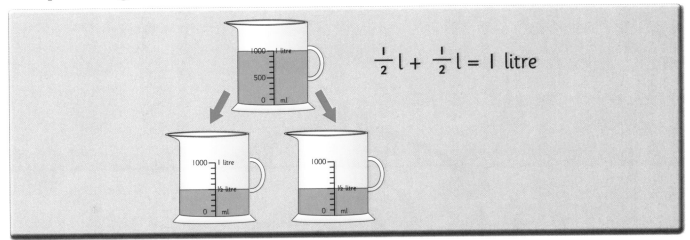

$$\frac{1}{2}l + \frac{1}{2}l = 1 \text{ litre}$$

1. **Estimate and measure the capacity of each container.**

container	estimates			The correct answer was . . .
	less than $\frac{1}{2}$ litre	about $\frac{1}{2}$ litre	more than $\frac{1}{2}$ litre	
glass				
mug				
butter tub				
saucepan				

2. **At home. Draw a container that holds these amounts.**

holds less than $\frac{1}{2}$ litre	holds about $\frac{1}{2}$ litre	holds more than $\frac{1}{2}$ litre

Capacity – $\frac{1}{4}$ Litre

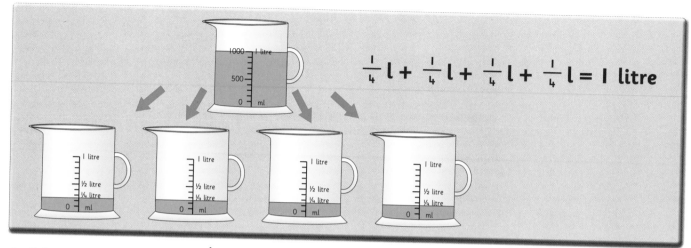

$\frac{1}{4}l + \frac{1}{4}l + \frac{1}{4}l + \frac{1}{4}l = 1$ litre

1. **Now investigate $\frac{1}{4}$ litre by estimating, measuring and recording your results.**

container	my estimates			The correct answer was . . .
	less than $\frac{1}{4}$ litre	about $\frac{1}{4}$ litre	more than $\frac{1}{4}$ litre	
juice carton				
jug				
sugar bowl				
soup bowl				

2. **At home. Draw containers that hold these amounts.**

holds less than $\frac{1}{4}$ litre	holds about $\frac{1}{4}$ litre	holds more than $\frac{1}{4}$ litre

1. **Colour to show the different capacities on each jug.**

1 litre	$\frac{1}{2}$ litre	$\frac{1}{4}$ litre	$\frac{1}{2}$ litre	1 litre
1 litre ½ litre ¼ litre 0 ml	1 litre ½ litre ¼ litre 0 ml	1 litre ½ litre ¼ litre 0 ml	1 litre ½ litre ¼ litre 0 ml	1 litre ½ litre ¼ litre 0 ml

2. **At home. You will need:**

   - a teaspoon
   - a teapot
   - a bowl
   - a jug
   - a cup
   - a small empty yoghurt pot

3. a) How many teaspoons of water fill the yoghurt pot? ☐

   b) How many jugs of water does it take to fill the bowl? ☐

   c) How many cups fill the jug? ☐

   d) How many cups does it take to fill the bowl? ☐

   e) How many yoghurt pots fill the teapot? ☐

   f) How many bowls fill the teapot? ☐

   g) Which is better to fill the teapot?
   A teaspoon or a cup? ☐

   Why? _____

Capacity

The bucket holds 5 litres	The basin holds 2 litres	The sugar bowl holds $\frac{1}{4}$ of a litre	The mug holds $\frac{1}{2}$ a litre	The yoghurt carton holds $\frac{1}{4}$ of a litre

1. **Find the capacity**

a) 2 buckets ☐ l   b) 1 basin and 2 mugs ☐ l

c) 3 basins ☐ l   d) 1 bucket and 4 sugar bowls ☐ l

e) 4 yoghurt pots ☐ l   f) 1 mug and 2 yoghurt pots ☐ l

g) 1 bucket and 1 basin ☐ l

 Puzzler

A sink can hold 10 litres of water. If you used a jug that holds half a litre of water to fill the sink, how many jugs of water would you need?

Recap

• I can estimate and record the capacity of a container.
• I can choose the best measuring unit.
• I know all about the litre, $\frac{1}{2}$ litre and $\frac{1}{4}$ litre.

38. Money 2

This is a 2 euro coin
200 cents = 2 euros
200c = €2.00

 =

 =   ... (50 cent coins)

 =

 (10 cent coins)

1. **Make €2.00 in 6 different ways.**

2. **True or false? ✓ or ✗**

a) 50c + 50c + 50c + 20c + 10c = €2.00 ☐

b) €1.00 + €1.00 = €2.00 ☐

c) €1.00 + 50c + 50c = €2.00 ☐

d) €1.00 + 50c + 20c + 10c + 10c + 10c = €2.00 ☐

e) €1.00 + 20c + 20c + 20c + 20c + 20c = €2.00 ☐

f) 50c + €1.00 + 20c + 20c = €2.00 ☐

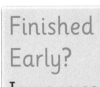

Finished Early?
In your copy, draw six different ways to make €3.00.

Strand: Measures
Curriculum Objective:
Exchanging and combining coins to the value of €2.

145

Money

1. How much?

 = 175c or €1.75

a)
133c

€1.33

b)
___c

___€

c)
___c

___€

d)
___c

___€

e)
___c

___€

f)
___c

___€

2. Match the amounts in cents to the correct price tag.

Remember: 136c = €1.36   213c = €2.13   6c = €0.06

39c €0.39
152c   €1.99
199c   €0.11
11c   €0.02
2c   €1.52

185c   €2.00
200c   €0.01
66c   €1.85
1c   €0.48
48c   €0.66

Puzzler

Which is the best value?
- 10 apples for €1.00   • 5 apples for 40c   • 20 apples for €2.00

Money
Change from €2.00

15c	20c	50c	€1.50	80c
45c	10c	70c	€1.00	60c

items bought	total cost	amount of money you have to spend	change
		€2.00	
		€2.00	
		€2.00	
		€2.00	
		€2.00	
		€2.00	
		€2.00	
		€2.00	
		€2.00	

Money Problem Solving

1.
Linda gets €2.00 each week for her pocket money.
Emma gets double that amount.
How much pocket money does Emma get?

€ [ ] + € [ ] = € [ ]

2.
I bought a book costing 95c and an apple costing 25c.
How much did I spend altogether?

[ ] c + [ ] c = [ ] c

3.
At the shops I bought some dog food which cost €1.70.
I paid with a €2 coin.
How much change did I get?

Change = [ ] c

4.
Tara bought a chocolate bar which cost 70c.
Kate's chocolate bar cost 50c more.
How much did Kate's chocolate bar cost?

[ ] c + [ ] c = € [ ]

5.
James bought 5 pencils, each costing 20c.
How much did he spend altogether?

[ ] c + [ ] c + [ ] c + [ ] c + [ ] c
= € [ ]

6.
Max wants to buy 3 buns.
They cost 25c each.
How much money does Max need to buy the buns?

[ ] c + [ ] c + [ ] c
= [ ] c

7.
Tom bought a toy train costing 42c, a lorry costing 25c and a car costing 31c.
How much did he spend altogether?

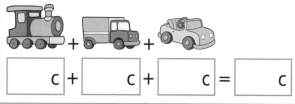

[ ] c + [ ] c + [ ] c = [ ] c

8.
Kim has €1.45. She wants to buy a scarf.
How much more money does Kim need to save?

€2.00

Answer: [ ]

Money

The bread costs €1.88 and you have €2. How much change will you get?
Count on to the nearest 5c or 10c.

€1.88

€1.88   +   €1.88   +   €1.90   +   €2.00

change

12c

1. Find the change from two euros (€2.00).

change

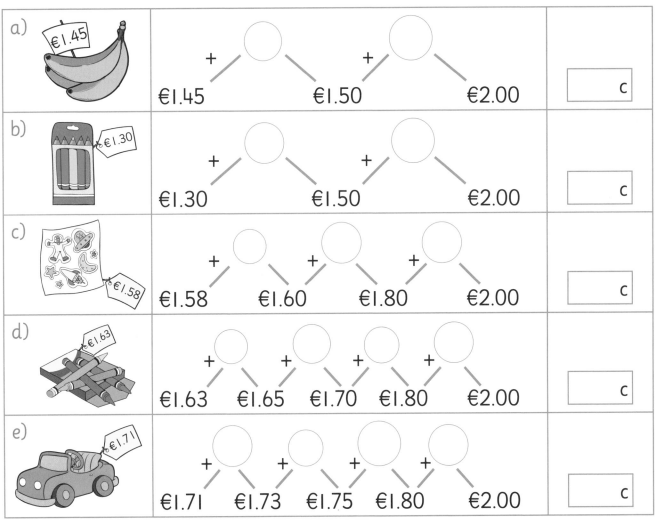

a) €1.45

+ ◯   €1.45   + ◯   €1.50   €2.00

☐ c

b) €1.30

+ ◯   €1.30   + ◯   €1.50   €2.00

☐ c

c) €1.58

+ ◯   €1.58   + ◯   €1.60   + ◯   €1.80   €2.00

☐ c

d) €1.63

+ ◯   €1.63   + ◯   €1.65   + ◯   €1.70   + ◯   €1.80   €2.00

☐ c

e) €1.71

+ ◯   €1.71   + ◯   €1.73   + ◯   €1.75   + ◯   €1.80   €2.00

☐ c

Recap

- I can recognise these coins.
- I can swap coins up to €2.00.
- I can find the cost of items and get the change.

39. Addition and Subtraction Word Problems

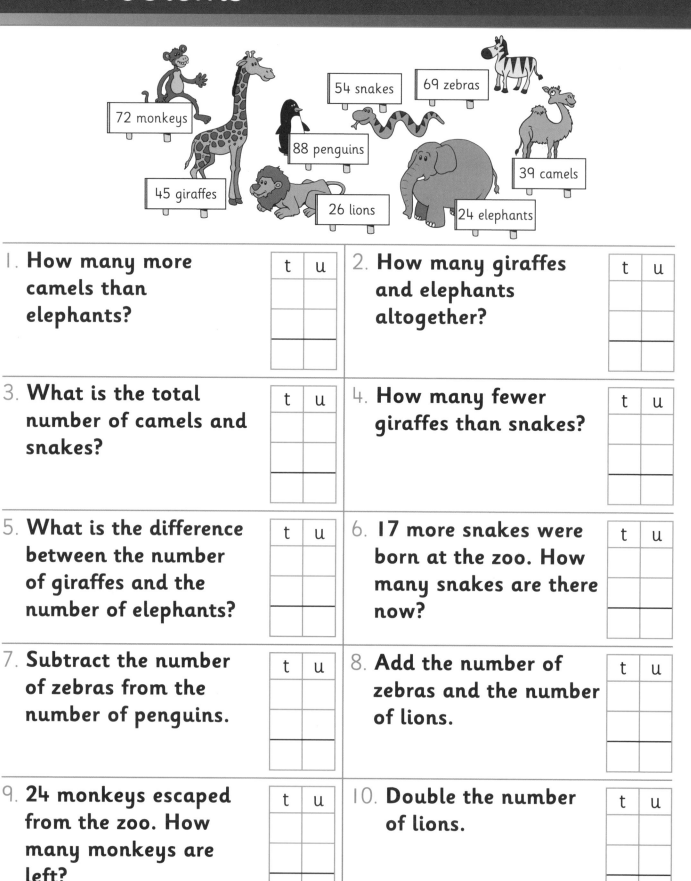

72 monkeys

54 snakes

69 zebras

88 penguins

45 giraffes

26 lions

24 elephants

39 camels

1. How many more camels than elephants?

t	u

2. How many giraffes and elephants altogether?

t	u

3. What is the total number of camels and snakes?

t	u

4. How many fewer giraffes than snakes?

t	u

5. What is the difference between the number of giraffes and the number of elephants?

t	u

6. 17 more snakes were born at the zoo. How many snakes are there now?

t	u

7. Subtract the number of zebras from the number of penguins.

t	u

8. Add the number of zebras and the number of lions.

t	u

9. 24 monkeys escaped from the zoo. How many monkeys are left?

t	u

10. Double the number of lions.

t	u

Strand: Number
Curriculum Objectives:
Add and subtract numbers without and with renaming within 99;

solve problems involving addition or subtraction; construct number sentences and number stories.

Add + or Subtract –

1. **Are you a good driver? Look at the signs carefully and add or subtract to get to the finish line.**

t u	t u	t u	t u	t u	t u	t u
6 5	3 4	7 2	5 4	7 4	2 8	6 5
+ 3 0	– 1 1	+ 2 1	– 2 2	+ 2 5	– 1 3	+ 2 4

t u	t u	t u	t u	t u	t u	t u	t u	t u
5 7	1 7	6 4	4 7	6 0	7 8	5 9	4 5	2 8
– 3 7	+ 7 8	– 6 4	– 1 5	– 5 7	– 1 0	+ 2 9	+ 1 6	+ 3 5

t u	t u	t u	t u	t u	t u	t u	t u	t u
5 7	1 7	6 4	4 7	8 1	7 8	5 9	4 5	2 8
– 2 9	+ 5 6	– 3 6	– 1 9	– 5 7	– 1 9	– 4 3	+ 2 9	+ 2 8

t u	t u	t u	t u	t u	t u	t u	t u	t u
4 7	1 7	9 0	6 7	6 0	1 4	5 5	4 5	2 8
– 3 7	+ 5 9	– 6 4	– 1 8	– 4 2	+ 4 2	+ 2 9	+ 3 4	+ 5 6

t u	t u	t u	t u	t u	t u	t u	t u
5 5	1 3	7 1	4 7	6 7	7 8	6 4	4 5
– 2 7	+ 6 8	– 6 4	– 1 9	+ 1 7	– 1 9	+ 2 9	+ 1 8

Solve the Riddles

1. What has a face but cannot see?

c	a	k	l	o
t u	t u	t u	t u	t u
2 0	3 9	4 6	2 9	2 5
− 6	− 1 5	+ 7	+ 5	+ 2 5

24		14	34	50	14	53

2. What gets wet when drying?

e	l	w	o	t	a
t u	t u	t u	t u	t u	t u
1 9	3 8	3 1	7 2	4 7	7 1
− 5	+ 2 6	+ 5 5	− 2 4	+ 4 8	− 2 8

43		95	48	86	14	64

3. What do you give a seasick elephant?

n	s	a	r	o	m	l	t	f	d
t u	t u	t u	t u	t u	t u	t u	t u	t u	t u
4 2	2 6	1 8	8 0	2 7	4 2	5 6	5 4	5 6	6 7
+ 3 7	− 1 3	+ 1 7	− 2 6	+ 5 7	− 1 4	− 3 9	+ 3 7	− 1 9	− 1 9

17	84	91	13	35	79	48	17	84	91	13	84	37	54	84	84	28

Two-step Number Stories

(26 + 12) − 14 = 24

```
  2 6        3 8
+ 1 2      − 1 4
─────      ─────
  3 8        2 4
```

1. Do the sum inside the brackets first.
2. Look carefully to see if you need to add or subtract.
3. Bring the answer of the first part to the top.
4. Do the second part to find your final answer.

1.

a) (37 + 10) − 12 = ____

t	u
3	7

+

1	0

t	u

−

1	2

b) (40 + 15) − 13 = ____

t	u
4	0

+

1	5

t	u

−

1	3

c) (25 + 13) − 21 = ____

t	u
2	5

+

1	3

t	u

−

2	1

d) (33 + 25) − 37 = ____

t	u
3	3

+

2	5

t	u

−

3	7

e) (26 + 49) − 14 = ____

t	u
2	6

+

4	9

t	u

−

1	4

f) (41 + 14) − 18 = ____

t	u
4	1

+

1	4

t	u

−

1	8

2. **Now try these. Be careful – this time we are not adding first.**

a) (76 − 15) + 31 = ____

t	u
7	6

−

1	5

t	u

+

3	1

b) (68 − 25) + 37 = ____

t	u
6	8

−

2	5

t	u

+

3	7

c) (98 − 27) + 14 = ____

t	u
9	8

−

2	7

t	u

+

1	4

d) (37 − 19) + 20 = ____

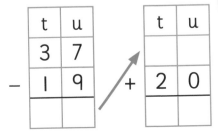

t	u
3	7

−

1	9

t	u

+

2	0

e) (45 − 28) + 37 = ____

t	u
4	5

−

2	8

t	u

+

3	7

f) (71 − 52) + 15 = ____

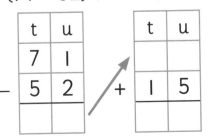

t	u
7	1

−

5	2

t	u

+

1	5

Word Problems

In the library there were 21 books on one shelf and 8 books on another shelf.
The children took 13 books home to read.
How many books were left?
1. Read the story carefully.
2. Decide if you want to add or subtract.
3. Write out the number sentence.
4. Estimate your answer.
5. Work out the part in the brackets first.
6. Then do the second part.

$(21 + 8) - 13 = \boxed{16}$

$$\begin{array}{r} 2\ 1 \\ +\ \ \ 8 \\ \hline 2\ 9 \end{array} \qquad \begin{array}{r} 2\ 9 \\ -\ 1\ 3 \\ \hline 1\ 6 \end{array}$$

1. Dan had 18 crayons in his pencil case. Mum gave him a new box with 25 crayons. He gave 12 of them to Jay. How many crayons had Dan then?

$(\quad + \quad) - \quad = \quad$

$$\begin{array}{r} 1\ \ 8 \\ +\ 2\ \ 5 \\ \hline \end{array} \qquad \begin{array}{r} \\ -\ 1\ \ 2 \\ \hline \end{array}$$

2. There were 26 blue cubes and 29 red cubes on the table. The teacher took 17. How many cubes are on the table now?

$(\quad + \quad) - \quad = \quad$

$$\begin{array}{r} 2\ \ 6 \\ +\ 2\ \ 9 \\ \hline \end{array} \qquad \begin{array}{r} \\ -\ 1\ \ 7 \\ \hline \end{array}$$

Now **you decide** whether to add or subtract. Put in the + or − sign.

3. There are 39 beanbags in one bag and 44 beanbags in another bag. 26 beanbags are used for PE.

   How many beanbags are not used?

$(\quad \quad) \quad = \quad$

$$\begin{array}{r} 3\ \ 9 \\ 4\ \ 4 \\ \hline \end{array} \qquad \begin{array}{r} \\ 2\ \ 6 \\ \hline \end{array}$$

4. There are 67 stars on the reward chart and 14 stars in the packet. Mrs Kelly puts 15 stars on the copies.

   How many stars are left?

$(\quad \quad) \quad = \quad$

$$\begin{array}{r} 6\ \ 7 \\ 1\ \ 4 \\ \hline \end{array} \qquad \begin{array}{r} \\ \\ \hline \end{array}$$

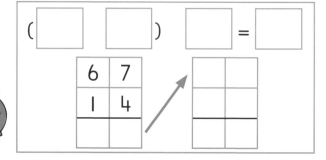

Addition and Subtraction Word Problems

1. **Write the numbers.**

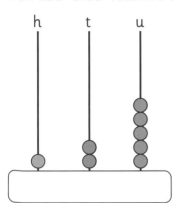
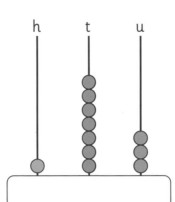
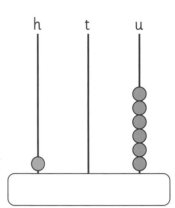

2. **Rename:**

47 = 3 tens and ☐ units   53 = 4 tens and ☐ units

3. **Fill in the missing numbers.**

	136

161		

123	

4. **Does a carton of milk hold 1 litre of milk or 1kg of milk?** _____

5. **Write the amount of money using the € sign.**

146c = € _____   193c = € _____   135c = € _____

6. **Mum bought a banana costing 35c and eggs costing 80c.**

How much did she spend altogether? ☐

7. **Dan got €2 from Gran. He spent €1.45 in the toy shop.**

How much change did Dan get? ☐

8. **Ann had 26 sweets in a box. Mum gave her 8 more. She ate 11.**

How many sweets are in the box now? ☐

Curriculum Objective:
To revise concepts that were explored in units 36–39.

C000078165

SQA QUESTION PAPER AND HODDER GIBSON MODEL QUESTION PAPERS WITH ANSWERS

NATIONAL 5

DESIGN AND MANUFACTURE

2013 Specimen Question Paper & 2013 Model Papers

This book contains the official 2013 SQA Specimen Question Paper for National 5 Design and Manufacture, with associated SQA approved answers modified from the official marking instructions that accompany the paper.

In addition the book contains model practice papers, together with answers, plus study skills advice. These papers, some of which may include a limited number of previously published SQA questions, have been specially commissioned by Hodder Gibson, and have been written by experienced senior teachers and examiners in line with the new National 5 syllabus and assessment outlines, Spring 2013. This is not SQA material but has been devised to provide further practice for National 5 examinations in 2014 and beyond.

Hodder Gibson is grateful to the copyright holders, as credited on the final page of the Answer Section, for permission to use their material. Every effort has been made to trace the copyright holders and to obtain their permission for the use of copyright material. Hodder Gibson will be happy to receive information allowing us to rectify any error or omission in future editions.

Hachette UK's policy is to use papers that are natural, renewable and recyclable products and made from wood grown in sustainable forests. The logging and manufacturing processes are expected to conform to the environmental regulations of the country of origin.

Orders: please contact Bookpoint Ltd, 130 Park Drive, Abingdon, Oxon OX14 4SE. Telephone: (44) 01235 827720. Fax: (44) 01235 400454. Lines are open 9.00–5.00, Monday to Saturday, with a 24-hour message answering service. Visit our website at www.hoddereducation.co.uk. Hodder Gibson can be contacted direct on: Tel: 0141 848 1609; Fax: 0141 889 6315; email: hoddergibson@hodder.co.uk

This collection first published in 2013 by
Hodder Gibson, an imprint of Hodder Education,
An Hachette UK Company
2a Christie Street
Paisley PA1 1NB

{BrightRED   Hodder Gibson is grateful to Bright Red Publishing Ltd for collaborative work in preparation of this book and all SQA Past Paper and National 5 Model Paper titles 2013.

Specimen Question Paper © Scottish Qualifications Authority. Answers, Model Question Papers, and Study Skills Section © Hodder Gibson. Model Question Papers creation/compilation, Answers and Study Skills section © Lindsay Bull. All rights reserved. Apart from any use permitted under UK copyright law, no part of this publication may be reproduced or transmitted in any form or by any means, electronic or mechanical, including photocopying and recording, or held within any information storage and retrieval system, without permission in writing from the publisher or under licence from the Copyright Licensing Agency Limited. Further details of such licences (for reprographic reproduction) may be obtained from the Copyright Licensing Agency Limited, Saffron House, 6–10 Kirby Street, London EC1N 8TS.

Typeset by PDQ Digital Media Solutions Ltd, Bungay, Suffolk NR35 1BY

Printed in the UK

A catalogue record for this title is available from the British Library

ISBN: 978-1-4718-0201-0

3 2 1

2014 2013

Introduction

Study Skills – what you need to know to pass exams!

Pause for thought

Many students might skip quickly through a page like this. After all, we all know how to revise. Do you really though?

Think about this:

"IF YOU ALWAYS DO WHAT YOU ALWAYS DO, YOU WILL ALWAYS GET WHAT YOU HAVE ALWAYS GOT."

Do you like the grades you get? Do you want to do better? If you get full marks in your assessment, then that's great! Change nothing! This section is just to help you get that little bit better than you already are.

There are two main parts to the advice on offer here. The first part highlights fairly obvious things but which are also very important. The second part makes suggestions about revision that you might not have thought about but which WILL help you.

Part 1

DOH! It's so obvious but …

Start revising in good time

Don't leave it until the last minute – this will make you panic.

Make a revision timetable that sets out work time AND play time.

Sleep and eat!

Obvious really, and very helpful. Avoid arguments or stressful things too – even games that wind you up. You need to be fit, awake and focused!

Know your place!

Make sure you know exactly **WHEN and WHERE** your exams are.

Know your enemy!

Make sure you know what to expect in the exam.

How is the paper structured?

How much time is there for each question?

What types of question are involved?

Which topics seem to come up time and time again?

Which topics are your strongest and which are your weakest?

Are all topics compulsory or are there choices?

Learn by DOING!

There is no substitute for past papers and practice papers – they are simply essential! Tackling this collection of papers and answers is exactly the right thing to be doing as your exams approach.

Part 2

People learn in different ways. Some like low light, some bright. Some like early morning, some like evening / night. Some prefer warm, some prefer cold. But everyone uses their BRAIN and the brain works when it is active. Passive learning – sitting gazing at notes – is the most INEFFICIENT way to learn anything. Below you will find tips and ideas for making your revision more effective and maybe even more enjoyable. What follows gets your brain active, and active learning works!

Activity 1 – Stop and review

Step 1

When you have done no more than 5 minutes of revision reading STOP!

Step 2

Write a heading in your own words which sums up the topic you have been revising.

Step 3

Write a summary of what you have revised in no more than two sentences. Don't fool yourself by saying, 'I know it but I cannot put it into words'. That just means you don't know it well enough. If you cannot write your summary, revise that section again, knowing that you must write a summary at the end of it. Many of you will have notebooks full of blue/black ink writing. Many of the pages will not be especially attractive or memorable so try to liven them up a bit with colour as you are reviewing and rewriting. **This is a great memory aid, and memory is the most important thing.**

Activity 2 — Use technology!

Why should everything be written down? Have you thought about 'mental' maps, diagrams, cartoons and colour to help you learn? And rather than write down notes, why not record your revision material?

What about having a text message revision session with friends? Keep in touch with them to find out how and what they are revising and share ideas and questions.

Why not make a video diary where you tell the camera what you are doing, what you think you have learned and what you still have to do? No one has to see or hear it but the process of having to organise your thoughts in a formal way to explain something is a very important learning practice.

Be sure to make use of electronic files. You could begin to summarise your class notes. Your typing might be slow but it will get faster and the typed notes will be easier to read than the scribbles in your class notes. Try to add different fonts and colours to make your work stand out. You can easily Google relevant pictures, cartoons and diagrams which you can copy and paste to make your work more attractive and **MEMORABLE**.

Activity 3 – This is it. Do this and you will know lots!

Step 1

In this task you must be very honest with yourself! Find the SQA syllabus for your subject (www.sqa.org.uk). Look at how it is broken down into main topics called MANDATORY knowledge. That means stuff you MUST know.

Step 2

BEFORE you do ANY revision on this topic, write a list of everything that you already know about the subject. It might be quite a long list but you only need to write it once. It shows you all the information that is already in your long-term memory so you know what parts you do not need to revise!

Step 3

Pick a chapter or section from your book or revision notes. Choose a fairly large section or a whole chapter to get the most out of this activity.

With a buddy, use Skype, Facetime, Twitter or any other communication you have, to play the game "If this is the answer, what is the question?". For example, if you are revising Geography and the answer you provide is "meander", your buddy would have to make up a question like "What is the word that describes a feature of a river where it flows slowly and bends often from side to side?".

Make up 10 "answers" based on the content of the chapter or section you are using. Give this to your buddy to solve while you solve theirs.

Step 4

Construct a wordsearch of at least 10 X 10 squares. You can make it as big as you like but keep it realistic. Work together with a group of friends. Many apps allow you to make wordsearch puzzles online. The words and phrases can go in any direction and phrases can be split. Your puzzle must only contain facts linked to the topic you are revising. Your task is to find 10 bits of information to hide in your puzzle but you must not repeat information that you used in Step 3. DO NOT show where the words are. Fill up empty squares with random letters. Remember to keep a note of where your answers are hidden but do not show your friends. When you have a complete puzzle, exchange it with a friend to solve each other's puzzle.

Step 5

Now make up 10 questions (not "answers" this time) based on the same chapter used in the previous two tasks. Again, you must find NEW information that you have not yet used. Now it's getting hard to find that new information! Again, give your questions to a friend to answer.

Step 6

As you have been doing the puzzles, your brain has been actively searching for new information. Now write a NEW LIST that contains only the new information you have discovered when doing the puzzles. Your new list is the one to look at repeatedly for short bursts over the next few days. Try to remember more and more of it without looking at it. After a few days, you should be able to add words from your second list to your first list as you increase the information in your long-term memory.

FINALLY! Be inspired...

Make a list of different revision ideas and beside each one write **THINGS I HAVE** tried, **THINGS I WILL** try and **THINGS I MIGHT** try. Don't be scared of trying something new.

And remember – "FAIL TO PREPARE AND PREPARE TO FAIL!"

National 5 Design and Manufacture

The exam

The following guidance will give you a clear plan to take into the examination room and help you achieve better grades. The Design and Manufacture examination is split into two sections.

Section 1

Section 1 is worth 24 marks and will ask questions based around the workshop manufacturing techniques that could be used to manufacture a simple product. All the questions in this section will be about the product and its component parts. It is likely that there will be a mixture of materials used in the manufacture of the product. Those materials will most likely be wood, metal and plastic.

A good examination preparation strategy would be to ensure you have knowledge of the properties of a range of softwoods, hardwoods, ferrous and non-ferrous metals, thermoplastics and thermosetting plastics.

In addition, you will need to be familiar with common workshop processes using these materials. The tools and equipment used with these materials are also areas which you should study. Remember – none of this is new to you and you will have spent time on the Design and Manufacture course making a range of projects from these materials. Be confident.

Section 2

Section 2 is worth 36 marks and will ask questions mainly about the design part of the course, though there will be around 6 marks worth of manufacturing questions, which will ask about manufacturing in industry.

The design questions will come from a range of topics which you will have covered in the course, such as the design team, the design process, design factors, sketching, modelling, product evaluation and specifications.

A simple word can be used to help you remember the design factors: **FEEDSCAMP**

Each letter stands for one of the design factors: **F**unction, **E**rgonomics, **E**nvironmental concerns, **D**urability, **S**afety, **C**ost (economics), **A**esthetics, **M**aterials and **P**roduction.

If you use this as a memory aid, you should be able to answer any question that asks about design factors. There are obviously additional areas contained within these headings, but it is a great help to have one word that reminds you of all the areas.

For the rest of the questions in this section, you should think back through your course and the work you did in the Design Unit. This should help you answer the questions about the design process, sketching, modelling, specifications and the product evaluation activities you were involved with.

Where marks are commonly lost

One of the major problems that markers find is the lack of description in students' answers. When asked about design factors in relation to a given product, such as a kettle, the usual response is:

'The kettle should be safe and durable.'

Although this is correct, we could be talking about any product on the planet, for example a watch should also be safe and durable.

To gain full marks, you should make clear reference to the product being asked about, so if we answer again about the kettle, the answer should be:

'It needs to be safe because the body of the kettle could get very hot with the boiling water and you could burn yourself. It needs to be durable because during the lifespan of a kettle it may get banged in the kitchen sink when being filled and it should withstand these collisions.'

When you look at the response above you can clearly see that we are talking about a kettle now and not a watch. Try to do this through the whole of the paper, specifically in Section 2 when each question is about a different product.

Another area where candidates answer poorly is within the product evaluation question. You should try to extend your answers to fully describe the activities you would carry out with reference to the product being asked about. Too often responses are simplistic, for example, when being asked about evaluating the ease of use of a vacuum cleaner:

'They should do a user trial.'

Or when being asked about value for money of a vacuum cleaner:

'They should do a comparison with other products.'

Once again, these answers are correct, but do not explain the activity in any detail and would therefore not attract full marks.

An exemplar answer would be:

'They should carry out a user trial, where a range of users vacuum an area of carpet and then describe how easy or difficult they found the vacuum cleaner to manoeuvre around small items of furniture.'

They should look at a range of existing vacuum cleaners that perform similar functions and see what their selling price is. They could then compare the selling price to theirs and this will show if their vacuum cleaner is good value for money.'

Where improvements could be made to achieve better grades

If you want to achieve a better grade you should think about the way you answer other questions, such as questions that ask for 'properties of materials that make them suitable for a particular product.'

If you try to explain the properties of HDPE it may be difficult and the ones you choose may not relate directly to the product being asked about. Try to list the properties the product needs to have to be successful at its function. If we take the example of a milk container made from HDPE, we can then say that HDPE can be recycled, it is available in a range of colours and it is non-toxic. These are all 'things' that the milk container does because it is a milk container not because it is made of HDPE. All of your properties of materials questions can be answered this way if you refer to 'what the product needs to do' rather than the material.

The ergonomics question is where you could rack up vital extra marks. This question can be answered in lots of ways, but it is a good idea to have a plan before you go into the exam in case the ergonomics question is in the paper.

Think about the three aspects of ergonomics: anthropometrics, physiology and psychology.

Try to write two answers for each area relating to the product in the question.

There is a simple formula to help you get full marks in this question.

For anthropometrics, pick a part of the product and then pick a part of the human body that should fit on/into that part. Link them together in a sentence and you get one mark. Do that twice to get full marks. E.g. Kettle: the handle of the kettle should fit the adult male palm width.

For physiology, pick a part of the product and then come up with a verb that you would do with that part. Link them together in a sentence and you get one mark. Do that twice to get full marks. E.g. Kettle: filling should be easy so the lid should be easy to open.

For psychology, pick a part of the product and then come up with a feeling or emotion to do with that part. Link them together in a sentence and you get one mark. Do that twice to get full marks. E.g. Kettle: the switch on the kettle should make a clicking sound to let you know that it is on.

Good luck!

Remember that the rewards for passing National 5 Design and Manufacture are well worth it! Your pass will help you get the future you want for yourself. In the exam, be confident in your own ability. If you're not sure how to answer a question trust your instincts and just give it a go anyway. Keep calm and don't panic! GOOD LUCK!

2013 Specimen Question Paper

FOR OFFICIAL USE

N5

National
Qualifications
SPECIMEN ONLY

Mark

SQ16/N5/01

Design and Manufacture

Date — Not applicable

Duration — 1 hour and 30 minutes

Fill in these boxes and read what is printed below.

Full name of centre

Town

Forename(s)

Surname

Number of seat

Date of birth

Day		Month		Year	
D	D	M	M	Y	Y

Scottish candidate number

Total marks — 60

SECTION 1 — 24 marks

Attempt ALL questions.

SECTION 2 — 36 marks

Attempt ALL questions.

Read every question carefully before you attempt it.

Write your answers, clearly in the spaces provided, using **blue** or **black** ink.

Show all working and units where appropriate.

Before leaving the examination room you must give this booklet to the Invigilator.
If you do not, you may lose all the marks for this paper.

MARKS | DO NOT WRITE IN THIS MARGIN

SECTION 1 — 24 marks

Attempt ALL questions

1. A pupil's project for a TV stand and storage unit is shown in the photo below.

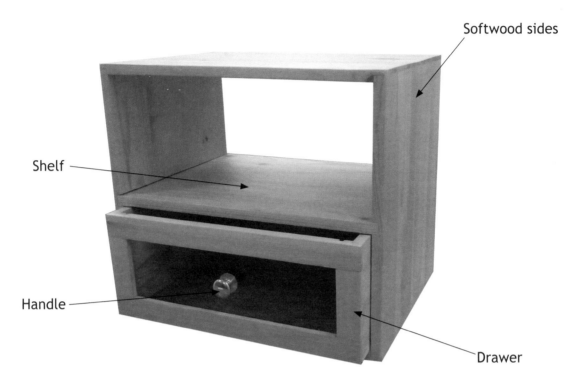

Softwood sides

Shelf

Handle

Drawer

(a) The base of the drawer was constructed from a manufactured board and the sides from softwood.

    (i) State the name of a suitable manufactured board for the base of the drawer. **1**

_____

    (ii) Describe **three** benefits of using a manufactured board for the base of the drawer. **3**

_____

_____

_____

_____

_____

MARKS | DO NOT WRITE IN THIS MARGIN

1. (a) (continued)

(iii) Describe **two** sustainability issues that may have made softwood the preferred material for the sides of the TV stand.   2

_____

_____

_____

(b) The photo below shows the joint in the side of the TV stand used to hold the shelf.

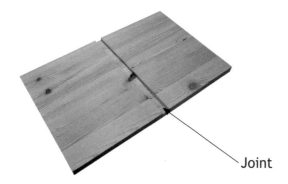

Joint

(i) Give a reason why the joint shown above is suitable.   1

_____

(ii) Describe **three** stages required to manufacture this type of joint using hand tools in a school workshop.   3

_____

_____

_____

_____

(c) Clear varnish was used as a surface finish for the softwood.

(i) Describe **two** benefits of using clear varnish as a surface finish for the softwood.   2

_____

_____

MARKS | DO NOT WRITE IN THIS MARGIN

1. (c) (continued)

(ii) Describe **two** stages in the preparation of the softwood before applying the varnish.

2

_____

_____

_____

_____

(d) The handle was made from a blank using a centre lathe similar to the one shown in the photo below.

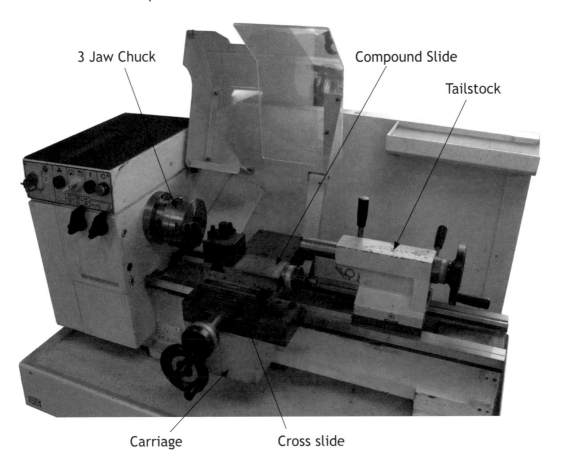

The handle consists of two parts as shown in the diagram below:

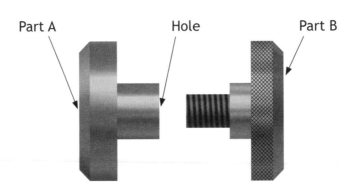

MARKS | DO NOT WRITE IN THIS MARGIN

1. (d) (continued)

Part B has been knurled.

(i) Describe the process of knurling on a centre lathe. **3**

_____

_____

_____

_____

(ii) State the functional reason for knurling Part B. **1**

_____

_____

_____

_____

Part A was created from a blank roughly sawn from a piece of aluminium bar as shown in the diagram below.

Original blank   Overall form of Part A

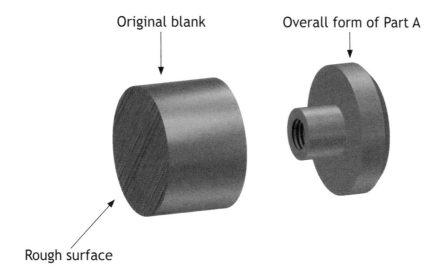

Rough surface

(iii) State **two** processes that would be carried out on a centre lathe to manufacture the overall form of Part A from a blank. **2**

_____

_____

_____

_____

MARKS | DO NOT WRITE IN THIS MARGIN

1. (continued)

The drawer of the TV stand contains a thermoplastic facing. The photos below show the piece of plastic cut to size and the rough edge of the plastic after sawing.

Plastic cut to size   Rough

(e) Describe **four** stages required to create a smooth surface finish on the sawn edges of the piece of plastic.   4

_____

_____

_____

_____

Total marks 24

MARKS | DO NOT WRITE IN THIS MARGIN

SECTION 2 — 36 marks

Attempt ALL questions

2.

The market for hairdryers has increased over recent years and designers have to consider various factors in their designs.

(a) Describe in what ways the design of hairdryers, as shown in the photo above, could have been influenced by ergonomics.

6

MARKS

2.   (continued)

(b) Before producing a design specification for a hairdryer, the designer would have researched various design factors.

Explain why the following design factors would be researched when designing hairdryers.

(i)   Aesthetics   1

_____

_____

_____

_____

_____

(ii) Performance   1

_____

_____

_____

_____

(iii) Materials   1

_____

_____

_____

_____

Total marks   9

MARKS | DO NOT WRITE IN THIS MARGIN

3.

Over recent years, there has been a steady increase in the number of electronic products available to consumers in the marketplace.

(a) Explain the term **"Technology Push"** with reference to **electronic products**.

2

_____

_____

_____

_____

_____

_____

All of the electronic products shown in the photo above were launched under a successful brand name.

(b) Describe **two** benefits to the designer of launching a product under a successful brand name.

2

_____

_____

_____

_____

_____

Total marks   4

MARKS | DO NOT WRITE IN THIS MARGIN

4. Designers often make models of their designs as they work through the design process as shown in the photos below.

Model of an iron

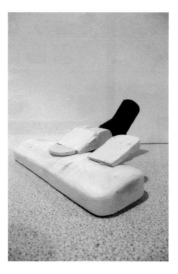

Model of a vacuum head

(a) Describe **two** benefits a designer could gain from modelling.

2

_____

_____

_____

_____

_____

_____

(b) State the names of **two** modelling materials and explain why **each** would be suitable for building models.

2

_____

_____

_____

_____

_____

_____

MARKS | DO NOT WRITE IN THIS MARGIN

4. **(continued)**

In addition to physical modelling, designers often use computer generated models as shown in the photos below.

Physical foam and card model

Computer generated model

(c) State **two** advantages to the designer of using a computer generated model rather than a physical model.   2

_____

_____

_____

_____

_____

Rapid prototyping is another type of model used by designers as shown in the photo below.

Rapid prototype of a mobile phone casing

(d) Describe **one** benefit that rapid prototyping offers the designer.   1

_____

_____

_____

Total marks   7

MARKS

5. A typical classroom chair is shown in the photo below.

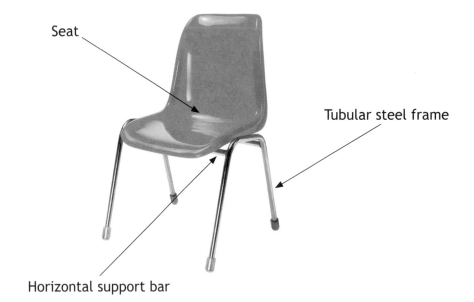

Seat

Tubular steel frame

Horizontal support bar

(a)   (i)   State the name of a suitable material for the seat of the chair.   **1**

_____

(ii)   Give **two** reasons why the material you have stated would be suitable for use in this type of product.   **2**

_____

_____

_____

_____

_____

_____

(iii)   State a suitable manufacturing process that could be used to manufacture the seat of the chair.   **1**

_____

MARKS | DO NOT WRITE IN THIS MARGIN

5. **(continued)**

Tubular steel was used to manufacture the frame of the chair.

(b) (i) State a joining technique that could be used to permanently join the horizontal support bars to the rest of the frame.   1

_____

    (ii) State the name of a suitable finish for the tubular steel frame.   1

_____

  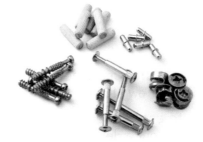

(c) Standard components, as shown in the photos above, are used in many products and are used to join the seat to the frame of the school chair. Explain **two** advantages to the manufacturer of using "standard components".   2

_____

_____

_____

_____

Total marks   8

MARKS | DO NOT WRITE IN THIS MARGIN

6. Two different types of coffee machines are shown below

Coffee shop coffee machine

Home coffee machine

The home coffee machine allows consumers to produce coffee shop style drinks in their own home.

In order to ensure the product would be a success, the designers would have had to carry out a detailed evaluation of the prototype.

(a) Describe **one** evaluation technique that may have been used when evaluating **each** of the following design factors.

(*Note: a different technique should be used for each factor.*)

(i) Ease of use   2

_____

_____

_____

_____

_____

(ii) Aesthetics   2

_____

_____

_____

_____

_____

MARKS

DO NOT WRITE IN THIS MARGIN

6. (a) (continued)

(iii) Value for money   2

_____

_____

_____

_____

_____

(b) Describe the roles of **two** design team members who would have been involved in the evaluation of the home coffee machine prototype.   2

_____

_____

_____

_____

_____

Total marks   8

[END OF SPECIMEN QUESTION PAPER]

2013 Model Paper 1

HODDER
GIBSON
LEARN MORE

National Qualifications
MODEL PAPER 1

Design and Manufacture

Duration — 1 hour and 30 minutes

Total marks — 60

SECTION 1 — 24 marks

Attempt ALL questions.

SECTION 2 — 36 marks

Attempt ALL questions.

Read every question carefully before you attempt it.

Write your answers clearly in the spaces provided, using **blue** or **black** ink.

Show all working and units where appropriate.

MARKS DO NOT WRITE IN THIS MARGIN

SECTION 1 — 24 marks

Attempt ALL questions

1. A small storage container is shown below.

(a) The container was manufactured mainly from softwood.

State the name of **two** suitable softwoods that could have been used.   **2**

_____

_____

(b) The back of the container is made from plywood as shown below.

Section 1 Questions (continued) **MARKS** DO NOT WRITE IN THIS MARGIN

(i) Describe the benefits of using plywood for the back of the container. **2**

(ii) State the name of **two** other manufactured boards that could have been used. **2**

(c) The drawer of the container is shown below.

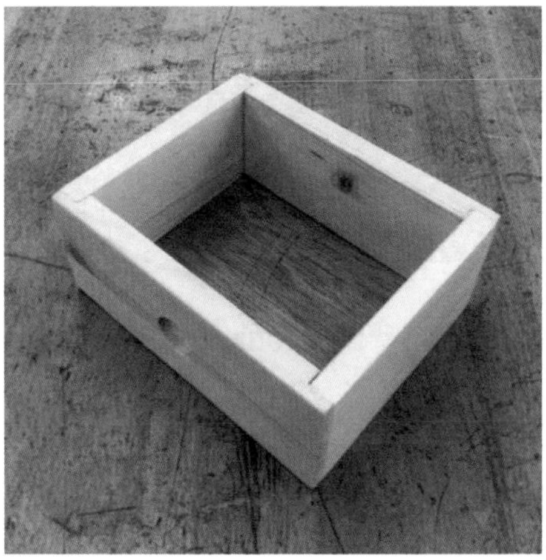

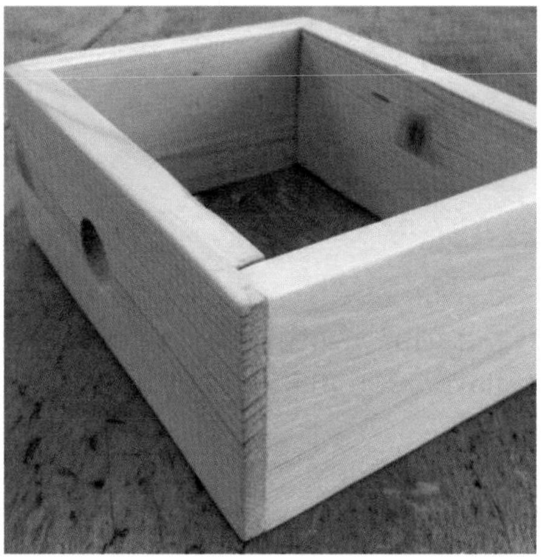

(i) State the name of **two** suitable joining techniques that could have been used at each corner of the drawer. **2**

(ii) Describe, with reference to tools, the way that one of the joints you have named above could be manufactured in the workshop using hand tools. **3**

The drawer has a 20mm diameter hole for opening instead of a handle.

(iii) Describe, with reference to tools and machinery, the way that the 20mm hole could have been manufactured in the workshop. **3**

Section 1 Questions (continued)

The container has been finished with wax.

(d) Describe the benefits of using wax to finish the surfaces of the container.   2

_____

_____

(e) The decorative plastic photo-frame shown below was added to the top of the container.

 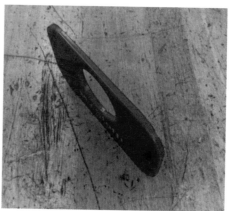

(i) Describe, with reference to tools, the way the four holes would have been marked out in the workshop.   3

_____

_____

_____

(ii) Describe the stages that would be carried out to make the edges of the plastic smooth and shiny.   4

_____

_____

_____

_____

The screws and eyelets used to join the plastic to the container were manufactured from a non-ferrous metal

(iii) State the name of a suitable non-ferrous metal.   1

_____

Total marks 24

SECTION 2 — 36 marks

Attempt ALL questions

2. Computer mice are shown below.

Before producing a specification for a computer mouse the designer would have researched various design issues.

With reference to a computer mouse:

State **four** design issues which would have been researched and explain why each of these design issues is important.

5

_____

_____

_____

_____

_____

_____

_____

_____

_____

_____

_____

_____

_____

Section 2 Questions (continued)

MARKS

3. A child's activity toy is shown below.

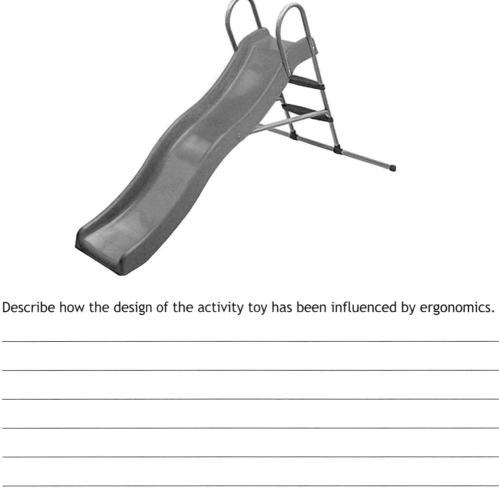

   Describe how the design of the activity toy has been influenced by ergonomics.   6

   _____

   _____

   _____

   _____

   _____

   _____

   _____

   _____

   _____

   _____

   _____

   _____

   _____

   _____

   _____

   _____

4. During the design process, a designer will use various materials to build models.

   (a) State **two** reasons why the designer would build models.   2

   _____

   _____

Section 2 Questions (continued) **MARKS** DO NOT WRITE IN THIS MARGIN

(b) State the name of **two** materials that could be used to produce models and explain why each material is suitable. **4**

(NB - A different explanation should be given for each material)

Total marks 6

5. A portable gas camping stove is shown below.

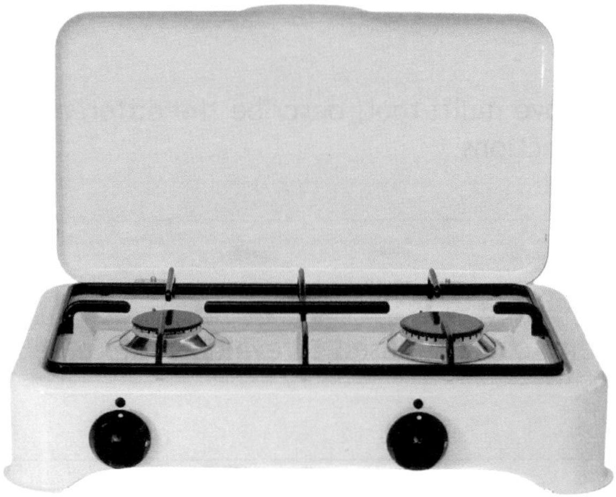

(a) Describe how each of the following issues has influenced the design of the camping stove.

(i) Environment **2**

(ii) Safety **2**

(b) The camping stove could be described as being attractive to a *niche market*. Explain the term *niche market*. **2**

Total marks 6

Section 2 Questions (continued)

6. A pocket multi-tool manufactured from stainless steel is shown below.

(a) With reference to the above multi-tool, describe the difference between primary and secondary functions.

2

_____

_____

(b) Describe a technique that could be used to evaluate the ease of use of the multi-tool.

2

_____

_____

(c) Describe the aesthetic qualities of the multi-tool.

2

_____

_____

(d) State **one** reason why the designer has chosen stainless steel for this product.

1

_____

_____

(e) State **two** methods of applying a coloured finish to the handles.

2

_____

_____

Total marks   **9**

Section 2 Questions (continued)

MARKS

7. The ability to generate ideas is an important aspect of a designer's work.

   (a) State **two** idea generation techniques.　　2

_____

_____

   (b) Describe how one of these techniques would be carried out.　　2

_____

_____

_____

_____

Total marks　4

[END OF PRACTICE QUESTION PAPER]

NATIONAL 5

2013 Model Paper 2

National Qualifications
MODEL PAPER 2

Design and Manufacture

Duration — 1 hour and 30 minutes

Total marks — 60

SECTION 1 — 24 marks

Attempt ALL questions.

SECTION 2 — 36 marks

Attempt ALL questions.

Read every question carefully before you attempt it.

Write your answers clearly in the spaces provided, using **blue** or **black** ink.

Show all working and units where appropriate.

HODDER
GIBSON
LEARN MORE

MARKS | DO NOT WRITE IN THIS MARGIN

SECTION 1 — 24 marks

Attempt ALL questions

1. A bird box is shown below.

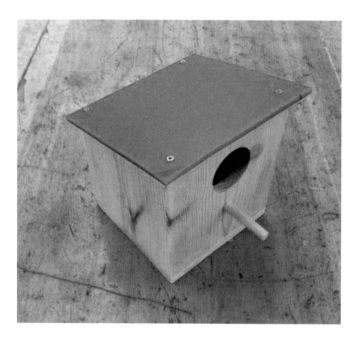

(a) The bird box was manufactured mainly from softwood.

    (i) State the name of a suitable softwood that could have been used in the manufacture of the bird box.

    _____   1

    (ii) Describe the environmental benefits of choosing softwood rather than hardwood.   2

    _____

    _____

(b) A peg has been fitted to the bird box as shown above.

    (i) Describe, with reference to tools, the way the position of the peg would have been marked out in the workshop.   3

    _____

    _____

    _____

    (ii) Describe a permanent method of joining the peg to the bird box.   3

    _____

    _____

    _____

Page two

Section 1 Questions (continued)

MARKS

(c) The corner of the bird box is shown below.

(i) State the name of **two** suitable joining techniques that could have been used at the corners of the bird box.

2

_____

_____

(ii) Describe the way that one of the joints you have named above could be manufactured in the workshop using hand tools.

3

_____

_____

_____

The bird box has a 35mm diameter opening to allow birds to enter.

(iii) Describe, with reference to tools and equipment, the way that the 35mm hole could have been manufactured in the workshop.

3

_____

_____

_____

_____

The bird box has been finished with clear varnish.

(d) Describe the benefits of using clear varnish to finish the surfaces of the bird box.

2

_____

_____

Section 1 Questions (continued)

MARKS | DO NOT WRITE IN THIS MARGIN

(e) The roof of the bird box has been manufactured from plastic as shown below.

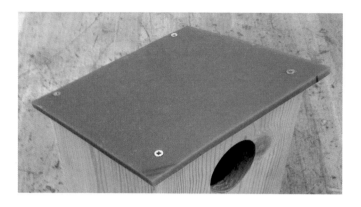

Describe the properties of thermoplastic that make it suitable for the roof of the bird box.   3

_____

_____

_____

_____

Screws were used to join the plastic roof to the main body of the bird box.

(f)   Describe an alternative method of joining the roof to the main body that would allow the bird box to be easily accessed for cleaning.   2

_____

_____

_____

_____

Total marks 24

SECTION 2 – 36 marks

Attempt ALL questions

MARKS

2. IPod docking stations are shown below.

Before producing a specification for an IPod docking station the designer would have researched various issues.

With reference to IPod docking stations:

State **four** design issues which would have been researched and explain why each of these design issues is important.

5

_____

_____

_____

_____

_____

_____

_____

_____

_____

_____

3. Designers use a variety of different graphic techniques in order to communicate.

State **two** graphic techniques, which the designer could use to effectively communicate with:

(a) The client

2

_____

(b) The manufacturer

2

_____

(c) Other designers

2

_____

Total marks   6

Section 2 Questions (continued)

MARKS | DO NOT WRITE IN THIS MARGIN

4. A toaster is shown below.

The manufacturer wishes to carry out an evaluation of the toaster.

Describe an evaluation activity that could be carried out for each of the following aspects of the toaster.

(NB - a different technique must be used for each aspect)

(a) Ease of use

2

(b) Aesthetics

2

(c) Value for money

2

(d) The speed of toasting

2

Total marks   8

Section 2 Questions (continued)

5. Children's cutlery is shown below.

Explain why the designer would consider **each** of following areas during the designing of children's cutlery.

(a) Ergonomics   1

_____

(b) Safety   1

_____

(c) Aesthetics   1

_____

(d) Materials   1

_____

                                                                       Total marks   4

Section 2 Questions (continued)

MARKS

6. The computer desk shown below was supplied as a flat-pack.

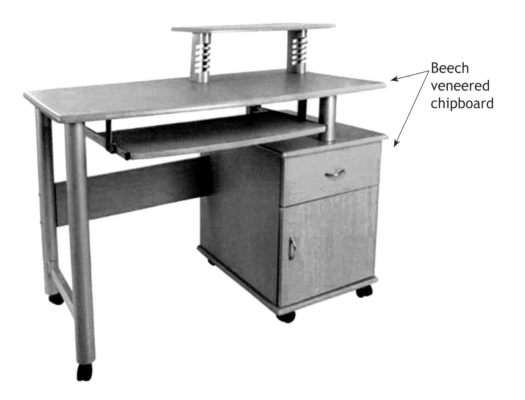

Beech
veneered
chipboard

(a) State **two advantages** to the **consumer** of flat-packed furniture.   2

_____

_____

(b) State **two** advantages of using beech veneered chipboard for the computer desk rather than using solid beech.   2

_____

_____

(c) Knock down fittings are often used in the construction of flat-packed furniture.

Explain the term '*knock down fittings*'.   1

_____

(d) Flat-packed furniture can be aimed at a particular market niche.

Explain the term '*market niche*' with reference to flat packed furniture.   2

_____

_____

Total marks   7

Section 2 Questions (continued)

7. A cordless vacuum cleaner is shown below.

Trigger

Dust collector

Nozzle attachments

Describe how the design of the cordless vacuum cleaner has been influenced by ergonomics.

6

_____

_____

_____

_____

_____

_____

_____

_____

_____

_____

_____

_____

_____

_____

_____

_____

_____

[END OF PRACTICE QUESTION PAPER]

NATIONAL 5

2013 Model Paper 3

HODDER
GIBSON
LEARN MORE

National Qualifications
MODEL PAPER 3

Design and Manufacture

Duration — 1 hour and 30 minutes

Total marks — 60

SECTION 1 — 24 marks

Attempt ALL questions.

SECTION 2 — 36 marks

Attempt ALL questions.

Read every question carefully before you attempt it.

Write your answers clearly in the spaces provided, using **blue** or **black** ink.

Show all working and units where appropriate.

DO NOT WRITE IN THIS MARGIN

SECTION 1 — 24 marks

Attempt ALL questions

1. A small display unit is shown below.

(a) The unit was manufactured mainly from pine.

   (i) State the name of one other softwood that could have been used in the manufacture of the unit.

   1

   (ii) Explain the reasons why designers often choose softwood rather than hardwood to manufacture products like the unit.

   2

(b) The main parts of the unit have been joined together using cross-halving joints.

Section 1 Questions (continued)

Describe, with reference to tools, the processes that would have been carried out in the workshop to manufacture the cross-halving joint.

3

_____

_____

_____

_____

_____

(c) The support used at the back of the unit is shown below.

A simple lap joint was used to join the two parts together.

Describe, with reference to tools, the way the lap joint could have been marked out in the workshop.

3

_____

_____

_____

_____

_____

Section 1 Questions (continued)

(d) The unit has two 6mm diameter metal uprights to support the front of the shelves.

(i) State the name of **two** suitable non-ferrous metals that could have been used.

2

_____

_____

The metal has been cut from a long section of bar to 130mm long.

(ii) Describe, with reference to tools, the processes that could have been used to mark out and cut the bar to length in the workshop.

3

_____

_____

_____

_____

_____

(iii) After the bars have been cut, the ends could be sharp and unsafe.

Describe, with reference to tools the processes that could be used to smooth the ends of the bars to make them safe.

3

_____

_____

_____

_____

_____

Section 1 Questions (continued)   MARKS

     (iv) Describe a method of permanently joining the metal bars to the wooden shelves.   2

_____

_____

_____

_____

_____

_____

(e) Before applying wax as a finish to the wood, the surfaces would need to be prepared.

Describe the processes that could be carried out to ensure the surfaces were ready to be waxed.   3

_____

_____

_____

_____

_____

_____

(f) Describe the benefits of using wax to finish the wooden surfaces of the unit.   2

_____

_____

_____

_____

_____

_____

Total marks 24

SECTION 2 — 36 marks

Attempt ALL questions

MARKS

2. Salt and pepper sets are shown below.

 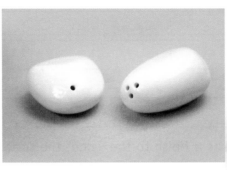 

Before producing a specification for a salt and pepper set the designer would have researched various issues.

State **four** design issues which would have been researched and explain why each of these design issues is important.

5

_____

_____

_____

_____

_____

_____

_____

_____

_____

_____

Section 2 Questions (continued)

MARKS

3.   A pair of training shoes is shown below.

(a)   Describe how consumer demand influences the design of training shoes.   2

_____

_____

_____

_____

_____

(b)   Advertising is one technique used to increase sales of training shoes.

Describe **two** other techniques which could also be used to increase sales.   4

_____

_____

_____

_____

_____

Total marks   6

4. A CAD model of a proposed printer design is shown below.

MARKS | DO NOT WRITE IN THIS MARGIN

The manufacturer wishes to carry out market research activities about the printer.

(a) Describe an activity that could be carried out for each of the following aspects of the proposed printer.

(NB - a different activity must be used for each aspect)

   (i) Value for money

                                                                            2

   (ii) Aesthetics

                                                                            2

Section 2 Questions (continued)   MARKS

(b) Describe the advantages to the manufacturer of using CAD modelling during the design of the printer.   **3**

_____

_____

_____

(c) State **three** techniques (**other than CAD modelling**), which the designer could use to effectively communicate with other members of the design team.   **3**

_____

_____

_____

Total marks 10

5. The ability to generate ideas is an important aspect of a designer's work.

(a) State **two** idea generation techniques.   **2**

_____

_____

(b) Describe how one of the techniques you have named above would be carried out by the designer.   **2**

_____

_____

_____

_____

_____

_____

Total marks   4

Section 2 Questions (continued)

MARKS | DO NOT WRITE IN THIS MARGIN

6. Five products are shown below with a list of manufacturing processes.

   Match each product or part of product with the most suitable manufacturing process from the list.

| A | Oil tank

| B | Table leg

| C | Metal parasol stand

| D | Houehold guttering

| E | Metal muffin tray

- **Manufacturing Processes**
- Soldering
- Rotational Moulding
- Press-forming
- Extrusion
- Compression moulding
- Injection moulding
- Sand casting
- Laminating
- Turning

(a) _____ **1**

(b) _____ **1**

(c) _____ **1**

(d) _____ **1**

(e) _____ **1**

Total marks 5

Section 2 Questions (continued)

7.   A hand held game is shown below.

Describe how the design of the hand held game has been influenced by ergonomics.

_____

_____

_____

_____

_____

_____

_____

_____

_____

_____

_____

_____

_____

_____

_____

Total marks   6

[END OF PRACTICE QUESTION PAPER]

SQA AND HODDER GIBSON NATIONAL 5 DESIGN AND MANUFACTURE 2013

Section 1

1. (a) (i) Any one of the following:
   - Hardboard
   - Plywood
   - MDF
   (ii) A description that covers three of the following benefits:
   - Low cost
   - Strong (enough)
   - Uses recycled materials
   - Available in large boards
   - Can be cut to any shape
   - Easy to machine
   - Uniform thickness
   - Durable
   - Readily available
   - Any other suitable response
   (iii) A description that covers two of the following issues:
   - Softwood trees grow faster
   - Softwoods grow in farmed forests
   - Using hardwoods endangers rainforests

   (b) (i) It supports the shelf across its width.
   (ii) A description that covers the following three stages:
   - Marking out two parallel lines and required depth
   - Cutting slot between the two parallel lines
   - Levelling the slot to a consistent depth

   (c) (i) A description that covers two of the following benefits:
   - Enhances appearance of softwood
   - Allows you to see the natural wood (unlike paint)
   - Hard surface protects against bumps/scratches
   - Hard surface protects against bumps/scratches
   - Prevents softwood drying out and splitting/warping
   (ii) A description that includes two of the following stages:
   - Remove pencil marks/blemishes with sandpaper
   - Wet wood to raise the grain
   - Sand lightly

   (d) (i) A description that includes the following three points:
   - Fit the knurling tool
   - Slow the speed of the lathe down
   - Slowly move the cross-slide towards Part B until it makes the knurled pattern to the required depth
   (ii) It provides grip for the user.
   (iii) Any two of the following processes:
   - Face off the ends
   - Chamfer the edge
   - Parallel turn the smaller diameter

   (e) A description that includes four of the following stages:
   - Through filing
   - Draw filing
   - Wet/dry paper
   - Emery cloth
   - Steel wool
   - Polish

Section 2

2. (a) *Anthropometrics:*

   The length of the handle will have taken into consideration the male 95th percentile dimension for hand width. This would ensure that as many people as possible could grip the handle comfortably.

   The designer would have to find the index finger width/circumference to determine the size of any switches or buttons to ensure as many people as possible could use the hairdryer with ease. If buttons are too small, people could find them difficult to locate and press.

   Physiology:

   The strength or power required to press the on/off button would have been considered to ensure users do not have to apply too much force. This excess force could result in the product being hard to use or even worse, causing injury.

   The strength or power required to operate the hinge of the green hairdryer would have to be considered by the designer. It needs to be easy to fold but not so loose as to fold during operation.

   The material used for the handles would have been considered to ensure the user can grip them comfortably. The user's hands could be damp from their wet hair so it is important that a slippery material is not selected.

   Psychology:

   A colour which contrasts with the main body of the hairdryer could be chosen to make the buttons stand out. This will make it obvious to the user which parts need to be pressed or adjusted to operate the hairdryer.

   A style or pattern on the hairdryer makes it appeal to a user's sense of style.

   (b) (i) Aesthetics would have to be considered when designing a hairdryer as it would have to appeal to the target market, whilst standing out against the competition.
   (ii) Performance would have to be considered when designing a hairdryer to ensure it safely dried hair in a reasonable amount of time.
   (iii) Materials would have to be considered when designing a hairdryer to make sure it did not heat up when in use and burn the user.

3. (a) An explanation that includes two of the following points.
   Products would be redesigned where:
   - Changes in manufacturing technology become available allowing electronic products to be manufactured at a lesser cost, more quickly or easily
   - Changes in materials technology become available allowing more complex or interesting shapes and forms to be manufactured, eg allowing them to be lighter, smaller, miniaturised, or more attractive to market
   - Changes in technology become available allowing electronic products to perform additional functions, eg motion sensors or GPS.

(b) Benefits of launching a product under a successful brand name are that it is:
  - Less risky for the designer
  - The brand will be recognised by consumers
  - People will be more willing to spend their money on the product if they have used the brand before
  - Successful brands have more money available for advertising.

4. (a) • Models will allow the designer to test/check the proportion and ergonomics of the product by allowing them to touch, hold and interact with it. They could then make changes as they develop the design further.
  • Models could be used to communicate the designs with other members of the design team. It may be easier for others to understand the design or parts of it in a 3D model rather than a sketch.

(b) Materials such as paper, card, MDF, wire, expanded foam, clay, balsa wood, sheet plastic could be listed. Reasons for suitability may include:
  - Low cost
  - Easy to work with and shape
  - Quick to work with
  - Give good results
  - Any other suitable answer.

(c) Possible advantages:
  - Time
  - Quality
  - Ease of communication between designers and offices, eg email
  - Ability to rapid prototype
  - Ability to add material surface effects
  - Can be used for marketing
  - Any other suitable answer.

(d) Possible benefits:
  - Quick to produce
  - Can be tested
  - Communication with design team and clients
  - Material finishes can be applied to make it look realistic
  - Can be used for marketing
  - Any other relevant answer.

5. (a) (i) Any one of the following:
  - Polypropylene
  - ABS
(ii) Reasons could include:
  - Strength and durability relating to repeated daily use
  - Strength to weight ratio relating to portability around school/class
  - Aesthetics—inbuilt colour, making it more attractive to the user
  - Cost—school budgets
  - Suitable for manufacturing process
  - Any other suitable answer.
(iii) Injection moulding

(b) (i) Welding
(ii) Suitable finishes:
  - Paint
  - Spray paint
  - Plastic dip coating

(c) An explanation that includes any two of the following points:
  - Cheaper than producing them yourself
  - Reliable
  - Variety available for different jobs
  - Secure fixing
  - Semi-permanent fixings
  - Any other suitable answer.

6. (a) (i) Ease of use:
  - A user trial could be used to evaluate the ease of use of the coffee machine. The designer may have asked consumers to make a cup of coffee whilst watching them to see if they had any problems in doing so. For example, finding switches, removing lids etc. Any problems noted could then be adjusted or changed before manufacturing the product.
(ii) Aesthetics:
  - A survey or questionnaire could be used to evaluate the aesthetics of the coffee machine.
  - Consumers could be shown a prototype of the product and asked their opinions on shape, form, colour, etc to ensure the designer has made it appealing to the target market.
(iii) Value for money:
  - A product comparison could have been used to evaluate if the coffee machine is good value for money. Similar products could be researched to find out how much they sell for, as well as the functions they offer. This would help give the team an idea of whether people would be willing to pay for their design or not.

(b) A description that includes any two of the following:
  - Market researcher/marketing team — would have been involved in evaluating how well the coffee maker met the needs and wants of the market or how competitively priced it is
  - Designer — would evaluate how well the design met the overall requirements of the design brief
  - Ergonomist — would have evaluated how easy the product was to use in terms of human factors, eg comfort, etc
  - Accountant — would have evaluated how financially viable the product would be, how much it has cost to design and produce
  - Retailer — would have evaluated how successful the product was in terms of sales.

NATIONAL 5 DESIGN & MANUFACTURE MODEL PAPER 1

Section 1

1. (a) Pine, Spruce.

   (b) (i) Plywood is strong in all directions and will not warp or bend after fitting.
      (ii) MDF, hardboard.

   (c) (i) Lap joint, dovetail joint.
      (ii) Lap joint: after marking out the joint with a try square, marking gauge and rule, you would cut down halfway through the wood with a tenon saw. Then you would chisel out the waste wood with a bevel edged chisel. Finally you could use a hand router to smooth the bottom of the lap joint.
      (iii) 20mm hole: after marking out with a rule and a try square, you would fit a forstener bit to the pillar drill. You would then drill slowly through the wood to make sure you don't split it at the back.

   (d) Wax makes the container look good and it also makes it more durable and helps to protect the wood from rotting.

   (e) (i) The four holes would have been marked out by using a rule, scriber and engineers square: the rule would be used to measure along the edge of the acrylic to the desired size, this would be marked by the scriber. Then the engineers square would be used with the scriber to mark out the positions of the holes.
      (ii) There are four usual stages, these are cross file, draw file, wet and dry paper or block and finally applying polish with a cloth.
      (iii) Brass.

Section 2

2. The designer would research: Function, ergonomics, durability and safety.
   - **Function:** The mouse will need to perform several operations such as scrolling and multi button use.
   - **Ergonomics:** The mouse will need to be the right size for most users' hands.
   - **Durability:** The mouse will need to be able to withstand being used every day and not wear away.
   - **Safety:** The mouse has some electrical connection and therefore it will need to be safe for the user to hold it and not get an electric shock.

   One mark for the four issues, one mark for each explanation.

3. Candidates have three possible routes to go down in their response.
   Anthropometrics, physiology and psychology. There is no requirement to refer to any of these areas by name. Typical responses within each aspect are shown below. Six suitable responses will gain six marks. Any suitable answer relating human dimensions and relevant aspect of the activity toy should be awarded one mark. e.g. The slide width has been designed to suit child hip breadth.

   Other suitable answers:
   - Width/length of treads — body/foot/leg width
   - Diameter of ladder frame — grip diameter
   - Vertical distance between treads — leg stretch
   - Height of handrail — arm reach/stretch

Any suitable answer relating to human limitations, linking to part of the activity toy should be awarded one mark.

The use of physical action verbs linking to the use of the activity toy are to be looked for here. E.g. the activity toy has been designed to be moved easily by an adult around the garden.

Other suitable answers:

The activity toy — moving, lifting, dragging, shifting

Tread spacing — leg raise, climbing

Any suitable answer relating to human thoughts/feelings/ emotions, linking to part or bit of the activity toy should be awarded one mark.

E.g. the choice of bright/warm/advancing coloured material on the slide will ensure that the user knows which part is the fun part.

Other suitable answers:
Bumpy appearance — fun/exciting
Robust appearance — feeling of safety (for child/parent/ carer)/ stability
Bright colours — fun

4. (a) • Models are used to develop an idea by giving a three dimensional view of a concept
      • Models can be used to test for ergonomic and aesthetic decision making.

   One mark per correct response up to total of two marks.

   (b) Possible materials range from modelling clay through to wire, plywood, acrylic and smart modelling materials.

   One mark awarded for the correct naming of each modelling material.

   One mark should be awarded for suitable justification of each modelling material e.g. modelling clay: because it can be remoulded many times.

5. (a) (i) Note; Environment here could mean either its working environment or its effect on the environment as a whole.
         Description of environmental issues could include:
         • Weather factors affecting its operation
         • Properties of materials factors, corrosion etc
         • Carbon footprint
         • Awareness of potential fire risk to the local environment
         • Ease of cleaning
         • Ease of maintenance
         • Any other reasonable response.

   Any two described environmental issues for one mark each.

      (ii) Description of safety issues could include:
         • Safety of user
         • Stability
         • Safety to local environment
         • Properties of materials relating to safety, heat etc
         • Hot surfaces
         • Use of gas
         • Any other reasonable response.

   Any two described safety issues for one mark each.

(b) Explanation should consider the following issues:
  - Identifying a need that is not being addressed by mainstream providers
  - Narrowly defined group of potential customers
  - Demand for a product that is not satisfactorily being met
  - Small in comparison to the mainstream marketplace
  - Specialization on small identifiable market areas
  - Any other reasonable response.

Any two explained issues for one mark each.

6. (a) • Primary functions versus secondary functions.
  - Pocket tool — scissors and various functions. Original tools had one function — multi-tool has several.
  - One main function plus additional uses or features.

Two marks will be awarded for a described, clear answer.

(b) • User trial, user trip, observation, user questionnaire.

No marks for naming the technique, only for the description.

Two marks will be awarded for a described, clear answer.

(c) Shape of handles, curved lines, contrast in colours, logo stylish, plastic versus stainless steel, wow factor.

Two marks will be awarded for a described, clear answer.

(d) Justified reason for stainless steel in context of this product.
  - strength/hardness/durability

One justified reason for one mark.

(e) • Dip coat, powder coat, electro plating, spray painting

Two methods for one mark each.

7. (a) Morphological analysis, design stories.

One mark per correct response up to a total of two marks

(b) Design Stories: to generate ideas using design stories you would put yourself in the place of the product you are designing. You would write a short story about a day in the life of the product or a story about the product being used. This then gives you a few ideas about what the product might need to do. This helps write the specification, which will lead to a range of ideas.

NATIONAL 5 DESIGN & MANUFACTURE MODEL PAPER 2

Section 1

1. (a) (i) Pine
    (ii) It can be locally sourced and it comes from sustainable forests.

  (b) (i) The position of the peg would have been marked out by using a rule, pencil and try square. The rule would be used to measure along the edge of the piece of wood to the required dimension; this would be marked by the pencil. Then the try-square would be used with the pencil to mark lines at 90 degrees to the edge of the wood. This would then be measured and marked along to get the position of the peg.
    (ii) The peg would be joined to the box using PVA glue and a blind hole. The hole would be drilled using a hand drill or pillar drill.

  (c) (i) Lap joint, dovetail joint.
    (ii) Lap joint: after marking out the joint with a try square, marking gauge and rule, you would cut down halfway through the wood with a tenon saw. Then you would chisel out the waste wood with a bevel edged chisel. Finally you could use a hand router to smooth the bottom of the lap joint.
    (iii) 35mm hole: after marking out with a rule and a try square, you would fit a forstener bit or flat bit to the pillar drill. You would then drill slowly through the wood to make sure you don't split it at the back.

  (d) Varnish makes the box look good and it also makes it more durable and helps to protect the wood from rain and other weather conditions.

  (e) Thermoplastic can be worked with and easily cut to size. It is also available in colours, such as green, which look good in an outdoors environment. It is also weatherproof and will not rot or fade in the outdoors.

  (f) A wooden insert could be fitted to the inside of the roof which fits tightly into the internal space of the box. This would allow the roof to be lifted off easily and would add to the weight of the thermoplastic so it did not blow away.

Section 2

2. The designer would research: **Function**, **ergonomics**, **durability** and **safety**.

  - **Function:** Function is important because the designer needs to find out what the docking station could do. Such as volume and tone settings for the music.
  - **Ergonomics:** The buttons need to be easily pressed and fit human hand sizes.
  - **Durability:** The materials used to make the docking station should withstand regular use, such as buttons or controls.
  - **Safety:** The connections to the power source should be safe and not endanger the user from electric shock.

One mark for the four issues, and one mark for each explanation

3. (a) **The client:** Presentation drawing, Pictorial drawings.
  (b) **The manufacturer:** Orthographic drawing, Exploded view.
  (c) **Other designers:** Initial sketches, developed design details.

4. (a) **Ease of use:** user trial — toast a piece of bread and describe how easy it was to use the toaster.

(b) **Aesthetics:** survey — ask a group of people if they like the colour used in the design of the toaster.

(c) **Value for money:** comparison to other products — compare the price of other products that do the same job and see if the toaster is a reasonable selling price.

(d) **Speed of toasting:** testing — time the toaster to see how long it takes to toast the bread and compare to other toasters.

5. (a) **Ergonomics:** any relevant and true anthropometric, psychological or physiological explanation.

(b) **Safety:** sharpness/bluntness/build quality/hygiene/weight/etc.

(c) **Aesthetics:** shape/size/form/contrast/colour/encourage usage/etc.

(d) **Materials:** comfortable/tactile/attractive or in-built colour/hygiene/safety/ease of cleaning/lightweight/non-allergenic/etc.

6. (a) Instant purchase
Easy to assemble
No delivery waiting
Low cost
Satisfaction of building
Easy to transport
Easy to store prior to assembly
Disassembly option, when not in use
Access to difficult property areas, such as up narrow staircases.

(b) Low cost
Environmental reasons
Uniformity of thickness
Smooth surfaces
Easy to machine
Wide flat boards
Knock Down Fittings are compatible
Uses materials that might be considered as waste.

(c) Special fittings to join furniture parts together
Mechanical fixing using standard components

(d) A market niche is a particular group of people that a product could be aimed towards. Flat pack furniture is low cost and has a limited life span. Young families with less income would be the ideal market niche for flat pack furniture.

7. Candidates have three possible routes to go down in their response.
Anthropometrics, physiology and psychology.

There is no requirement to refer to any of these areas by name. Typical responses within each aspect are shown below. Six suitable responses will gain six marks.

Any suitable answer relating human dimensions and relevant aspect of the vacuum cleaner should be awarded one mark, e.g. the handle length has been designed to suit adult male 95th percentile palm width.

Other suitable answers:
Trigger size — fingertip width
Gap between handle and main body — adult hand thickness.

Any suitable answer relating to human limitations, linking to part of the activity toy should be awarded one mark.

The use of physical action verbs linking to the use of the vacuum cleaner are to be looked for here, e.g. the vacuum cleaner is lightweight so it can be moved easily by an adult around the house.

Other suitable answer:
The controls — easily turned/pressed/switched.

Any suitable answer relating to human thoughts/feelings/emotions, linking to part or bit of the vacuum cleaner should be awarded one mark. E.g. the choice of white coloured material on the cleaner will make the user feel it is a hygienic product to use.

Other suitable answer:
Contrasting red and white — shows you where the uses can move or adjust and switch things.

NATIONAL 5 DESIGN & MANUFACTURE MODEL PAPER 3

Section 1

1. (a) (i) Spruce
   (ii) They look modern and are environmentally friendly.

   (b) The cross halving joint would be marked out and then you could use a tenon saw to saw down halfway through the wood. A bevel edged chisel could then be used to remove the waste wood. This would be repeated on the other piece of wood. The two parts would then fit together making the halving joint.

   (c) A try-square, marking gauge, rule and pencil would be used to mark out the lap joint. The rule would be used to measure along the edge of the wood to the required dimension. The try-square would be used to mark the lines at 90 degrees to the edge and the marking gauge would be used to mark along the grain to join up with the try-square lines.

   (d) (i) Aluminium, brass.
   (ii) The bar would be marked out using a rule, scriber and engineer's square. It could then be cut to size using a hacksaw.
   (iii) The bar would be put in an engineer's vice and filed smooth with a flat file. Emery cloth could then be used to smooth the filed surface.
   (iv) A 6mm hole could be drilled into the piece of wood on the pillar drill using a twist drill. Epoxy resin glue could then be used to permanently secure the metal in the hole.

   (e) The surfaces of wood would be sanded using sandpaper to remove pencil lines, excess glue and any dirty marks. The dust from sanding would then be removed using white spirit. The surfaces would then be ready for sanding.

   (f) Wax makes the unit look good and it also makes it more durable and helps to protect the wood from damage when items are placed onto it.

Section 2

2. The designer would research: **Function**, **ergonomics**, **durability** and **sustainability**.

   Function: they would want to know what the main job of the grinders would be; would they need to be adjustable?
   Ergonomics: they would need to know what sizes of the human body are important such as grip diameter.
   Durability: they would need to know about different materials and what possible dangers they would need to withstand in a kitchen environment.
   Sustainability: they would need to find out about the types of materials or woods that could be locally sourced and are sustainable to appeal to the environmentally aware customer.

   One mark for the four issues, one mark for each explanation.

3. (a) Consumers need to have a trainer that is fashionable and also comfortable to wear. This leads the manufacturers to make trainers that are both.

   (b) They could offer a special discount on gym membership if you buy a pair of trainers of that brand.

   They could give you a chance to win a trip to the next Olympics by asking you to phone a hotline with a code in your shoe box. This would increase sales.

4. (a) (i) The selling cost of the printer could be compared to other printers on the market and a decision could be made as to the value for money compared to the other printers.
   (ii) A survey could be carried out asking the public what their opinion of the colours used in the design of the printer. This could then lead to other colours being available.

   (b) CAD modelling is very quick and accurate and drawings can be altered very easily without a great deal of time being taken by the designer.

   (c) A model made out of resistant materials such as Styrofoam
   A working drawing with dimensions
   A final presentation drawing with the environment of the printer shown.

5. (a) Morphological analysis, design stories.
   One mark per correct response up to total of two marks.

   (b) Morphological Analysis: MA is a technique that you use to generate ideas by making columns of words from which you can pick random selections. The columns are under different headings like shape, colour and theme. This gives you a range of aspects to include in your idea.

6. (a) Rotational moulding

   (b) Turning

   (c) Sand Casting

   (d) Extrusion

   (e) Press-forming

7. Candidates have three possible routes to go down in their response — anthropometrics, physiology and psychology.

   There is no requirement to refer to any of these areas by name. Typical responses within each aspect are shown below. Six suitable responses will gain six marks.

   Any suitable answer relating human dimensions and relevant aspect of the hand held game should be awarded one mark, e.g. the buttons have been designed to suit children's finger tip sizes.

   Other suitable answer:
   Pointer diameter — child grip diameter

   Any suitable answer relating to human limitations, linking to part of the hand held game should be awarded one mark.

   The use of physical action verbs linking to the use of the hand held games are to be looked for here, e.g. the hand held game screen is easy for a child to open.

Other suitable answer:
The buttons — easily pressed.

Any suitable answer relating to human thoughts/feelings/ emotions, linking to part or bit of the hand held game should be awarded one mark, e.g. the choice of the pink coloured plastic makes it look like it is designed for girls.

Other suitable answer:
Contrasting and pink and white — show you where the controls to work the game are.

Acknowledgements

Permission has been sought from all relevant copyright holders and Hodder Gibson is grateful for the use of the following:

The Perspex ® Trademark © Lucite International (SQP page 6);
Image © ppart/Shutterstock.com (SQP page 7);
Image © Plus69/Shutterstock.com (SQP page 7);
Image © forest_strider/Shutterstock.com (SQP page 9);
Image © Mr. Aesthetics/Shutterstock.com (SQP page 9);
Image © Jeremy Smith/Shutterstock.com (SQP page 9);
Image © photosync/Shutterstock.com (SQP page 12);
Image © Peter Polak/Shutterstock.com (SQP page 13);
Image © Madlen/Shutterstock.com (SQP page 13);
Image © DenisNata/Shutterstock.com (SQP page 13);
Image © George Dolgikh/Shutterstock.com (SQP page 14);
Image © nexus 7/Shutterstock.com (SQP page 14);
Photo of a BenQ computer mouse © BenQ Europe B.V. (Model Paper 1 page 5);
Fotolia 37832391: © photoshaker-Fotolia (Model Paper 1 page 7);
Photo of a Gerber multi-tool © Silva Ltd (Model Paper 1 page 8);
Photo of an intempo iPod docking station © Intempo, Ultimate Products Ltd. (Model Paper 2 page 5);
Photo of a Dualit toaster © Dualit Ltd (Model Paper 2 page 6);
Photo of a Black & Decker DustBuster CHV1500 © Black & Decker (Model Paper 2 page 9);
Fotolia 44425162: gleebpl-Fotolia (Model Paper 3 page 6);
Fotolia 13293392: © Tatesh-Fotolia (Model Paper 3 page 6);
Fotolia 49526034: © Tomasz Zajda-Fotolia (Model Paper 3 page 6);
Fotolia 3253692: © Alex-Fotolia (Model Paper 3 page 7);
HRF 4222788: © istockphoto/Greg Nicholas (Model Paper 3 page 8);
Photo of a Nintendo DS © Nintendo UK (Model Paper 3 page 11).

Hodder Gibson would like to thank SQA for use of any past exam questions that may have been used in model papers, whether amended or in original form.